already gone

Why your kids will quit church and what you can do to stop it

KEN HAM & BRITT BEEMER
WITH TODD HILLARD

Master
Books®

First printing: May 2009
Seventh printing: September 2010

ISBN-13: 978-0-89051-529-7
ISBN-10: 0-89051-529-8
Library of Congress Number: 2009900148

Unless otherwise indicated, Scripture quotations are from the New American Standard Bible.

Cover Design: jdausa.com, photo provided by potthaststudios.com
Interior Design: Diana Bogardus

Photo credit, p. 162–164: Dan Clymer, Restoration House Ministries

Please consider requesting that a copy of this volume be purchased by your local library system.

Printed in the United States of America

Please visit our website for other great titles:
www.masterbooks.net

For information regarding author interviews,
please contact the publicity department at (870) 438-5288.

Master
Books®
A Division of New Leaf Publishing Group
www.masterbooks.net

already gone

Why your kids will quit church and what you can do to stop it

Dedications

My parents, Elvin and Margaret Beemer, always told me they would rather see a sermon than hear one. My good friend Harold Anderson endured many challenges in recent years, but as each obstacle arose, his faith soared. I want to acknowledge and dedicate this book to Harold and to his enduring faith.

— *Britt Beemer*

I praise the Lord for the godly legacy of my parents who trained me to stand uncompromisingly and unapologetically on the authority of the Word of God. This book is not only a challenge from the authors, but from godly parents concerning what each one of us are doing toward preserving that godly legacy for subsequent generations.

Special thanks to my dear friends Jon and Sue Jones for allowing me sanctuary in their home to write my section of this book. . . .

And for the AiG donor who provided the funds for this valuable research.

— *Ken Ham*

Contents

Introduction

The large wooden doors shut behind me with a creak and a heavy thud. Outside, the incessant river of life continues to flow as millions of people jam the sidewalks and rush toward red double-decker busses. Beneath the streets, the London Underground moves the masses by the hundreds of thousands — like blood pulsing through the arteries of this vibrant, thriving society.

But inside, I can hear each of my careful footsteps echoing in the dim quiet. I inhale deeply, taking in the aroma of ancient stones and old books. I see rows and rows of ornate pews — seating for more than 3,000 — yet I am ushered into the small foyer area where around 30 chairs are set up and where I join a handful of elderly people with their heads bowed. Humbly and faithfully, those beside me say their prayers and listen to a brief message by a man who speaks of hope — but whose tired eyes seem to feel none of it.

It is Sunday. For hundreds of years the faithful have been walking through the heavy wooden doors on this day, at this time, to gather together and share in the timeless rituals of worship, prayer, and proclamation *that made this country the bastion of Christendom for centuries. But this morning I realize that I'm part of a funeral. But it is not the funeral of an individual; it is the funeral of an institution. Within months, the older generation will likely disband and the doors of this church will be shut and locked. The candles will never again be lit. The resounding anthem of the great hymns of our spiritual forefathers will never again echo in its passages.*

***

Since 1969, 1,500 churches in England have heard that final *thud* as their doors were shut after their final service after hundreds of years of active life.[1]

Most of the great churches still stand — grand buildings that just 60 years ago were the hub of vital and vibrant activity. Before World War II (and certainly during those turbulent years), churches such as the one I visited that day were the center of community and spiritual life. But now, the communities' life, such as it is, takes place outside of those buildings. Inside, many of them have become musty, dusty, and dark. The Victorian Society of the UK summarizes the situation in a publication entitled *Redundant Churches: Who Cares?*

> Invariably, it seems, churches become redundant. The country changes around them and for one reason or another they find themselves bereft of the worshippers needed to keep them going. Many, if not most, of the buildings seem eventually to find new uses, but it is not easy to generalize about how often these uses preserve their architectural and historic interest.[2]

It's not a small concern. Not far from the famous Westminster Abbey in London I found a sign that read: "Advisory Board for Redundant Churches."

---

1. The Victorian Society, No. 26, November 2007, http://www.victoriansociety. org.uk/publications/redundant-churches-who-cares/.
2. Ibid.

"Redundancy." The dictionary defines that word as "exceeding what is necessary or natural . . . needlessly repetitive." That is a disturbing term to describe a former place of worship, don't you think? Who cares about "redundant churches"? It seems not many these days. There are not many left to really care — except for those who see them for their "architectural" and "historical" value. Now emptied of their intended function, many also see the real estate value of these "needlessly repetitive" buildings. A special government agency oversees the distribution and preservation of these buildings. What does that sound like in formal language?

> The Redundant Churches Fund has as its object the preservation, in the interests of the nation and the Church of England, of churches and parts of churches of historic and archaeological interest or architectural quality, together with their contents, which are vested in the Fund by Part III of the Pastoral Measure 1983 (1983 No.1).[3]

In other words, if what's left has some value physically, it is sold or it is preserved. The rest is abandoned or bulldozed. What has become of the buildings worth keeping?

Other former places of worship have been turned into museums, clothing shops, music stores, liquor stores, nightclubs, and tattoo and piercing studios. One is even now used as a Sikh temple, and some have been converted into mosques.

Hundreds of these churches have ended up in the hands of private owners who convert them into offices or renovate them for use as personal homes or cottages.

It would be something of a relief if these former churches simply represented a shift from traditional worship toward more contemporary worship facilities, but that's not the case. The decline of the Church has followed the plummeting spirituality of a nation that has lost its roots — its foundation. England, the country that was once a cornerstone

---

3. http://www.opsi.gov.uk/si/si1994/Uksi_19940962_en_1.htm.

of western Christianity, is now, by and large, a wasteland of lost souls where the word "God" has many different definitions, with so few these days who would even think of "God" as the Creator God of the Bible.

According to a recent English Church Census:

- Regular churchgoers (of all denominations) amount to 6.3% of the total population.

- The proportion of churches per individuals is now one church to 1,340 people; the size of the average Sunday congregation, however, is 84.

- Between 1998 and 2005, there was an overall decline in regular church attendance of 15% — and the trend continues.

- 40% of regular churchgoers attend evangelical churches, but even these groups are seeing their numbers decline.[4]

All in all, only 2.5 percent of the population is attending Bible-based churches.

One United Kingdom news source in 2003 stated:

Holy Week has begun with an expert prediction that the Christian church in this country will be dead and buried within 40 years. It will vanish from the mainstream of British life, with only 0.5 percent of the population attending the Sunday services of any denomination, according to the country's leading church analyst . . . only 7.5 percent of the population went to church on Sundays and that, in the past 10 years — billed by the churches as the "Decade of Evangelism" — church attendance dropped by an "alarming" 22 percent.[5]

4. 2005 Evangelical Alliance, http://www.eauk.org/resources/info/statistics/2005 englishchurchcensus.cfm.
5. Ibid.

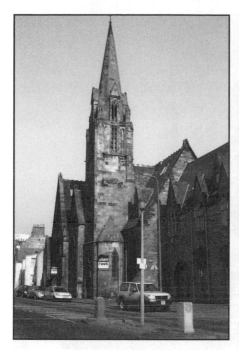

A church in the United Kingdom turned into a rock climbing center

A church (in John Bunyan's home town of Bedford, England) turned into a night club

A church in the United Kingdom turned into a theater

A church turned into a restaurant in the United Kingdom

A church in the United Kingdom
turned into a Sikh Temple

Another article in 2004 claimed: "Attendance at Britain's mosques has outstripped the number of regular worshippers in the Church of England for the first time. . . ."[6] I recently attended a church a couple hours north of London. It was a totally traditional Baptist service, but it was clear that it was a gathering of remnant believers from many backgrounds. It was a refreshing and unique sight to see excited people as the organ blasted out "The Old Rugged Cross"! Certainly, pockets of new life can be found, yet much of it is "imported." Since 2001, Africa has supplied the single largest pool of new British citizens, and many of the new arrivals bring with them the Pentecostal worship style that has drawn millions of Africans to Christian churches across the continent in the last several decades.[7] Other Bible-believing bodies of worshipers are holding their own and doing their best to reach out to the masses in this nation that now must be considered "post-Christian."

Empty churches now stand in the cities and the countryside as monuments to the triumph of the new religion of secular humanism. Hollow shells of buildings shadowing streets filled with hollow souls, the disease was the result of a predictable spread of ideas that seemed harmless enough to start with, and then mutated into a plague that killed the soul of an entire nation in two generations — and this same disease is being spread around the world. For instance, a news source in Australia quotes a university professor as saying, "Within the next 10–20 years, most of the main-line churches will be appropriately down on their knees praying for their own survival."[8]

Across the Atlantic, in the "One Nation Under God," the seeds of a free and God-fearing nation were planted only 250 years ago. Today, few people are aware of the spiritual epidemic that has wiped out the land of our Christian forefathers. England was the home of our great

---

6. "More Moslem Worshipers than Anglicans?" *British Church Newspaper*, February 20, 2004.
7. Associated Press, "Evangelicals Gain Strength in England, April 21, 2007."
8. Dr. David Tracy, associate professor, religion expert at Melbourne La Trobe University, quoted by Elissa Lawrence, "Losing Our Religion," *Sunday Mail*, Sunday Extra Section, Adelaide, Australia, December 29, 2002, p. 48.

spiritual ancestors — many of the greatest preachers, teachers, and evangelists of the last 200 years.

Few people are aware that the same epidemic has reached our own shores, spreading like an unstoppable virus.

When it comes to churches in America, our research shows that many are *Already Gone*.

A Heart for the Church

It is estimated that Ken Ham, president of Answers in Genesis and the new Creation Museum, has given more than 4,000 talks on the accuracy and authority of the Bible since 1973 (he started speaking full time in 1979) – plus has granted several hundred interviews with the world's media (NY Times, Washington Post, all the major US TV networks, the BBC several times, etc.).

Ken has given more biblical messages in various venues than an average pastor will give in a lifetime of sermons.

Among the many hundreds of churches in which he has spoken (in more than 20 countries), Ken has also spoken in some of America's largest and most influential churches – and thus has had his finger on the pulse of the church's health since moving to America in 1987:

- Calvary Chapel Costa Mesa, Calif. (Pastor Chuck Smith)—three times
- Harvest Christian Fellowship, Calif. (Pastor Greg Laurie)—three times
- Saddleback Comm. Church, Calif. (Pastor Rick Warren)
- Grace Community Church, Calif. (Pastor John MacArthur)—twice
- Thomas Road Baptist Church, VA (Pastor Jerry Falwell)—twice
- Bellevue Baptist Church, TN (Pastor Adrian Rogers)—twice
- First Baptist Church of Woodstock, GA (Pastor Johnny Hunt)—soon to be there a second time

Part 1:
An Epidemic on Our Hands

Epidemic (Ep-i-**dem**-ic)[1]

1. A disease or anything resembling a disease; attacking or affecting many individuals in a community or a population simultaneously.

2. Anything which takes possession of the minds of people as an epidemic does of their bodies; as, an epidemic of terror.

A majority of twenty-somethings — 61% of today's young adults — had been churched at one point during their teen years but they are now spiritually disengaged (i.e., not actively attending church, reading the Bible, or praying).

— George Barna[2]

1. Webster's Revised Unabridged Dictionary, © 1996, 1998 MICRA, Inc. , *Webster's Revised Unabridged Dictionary*. Retrieved December 09, 2008
2. http://www.barna.org/barna-update/article/16-teensnext-gen/147-most-twenty-somethings-put-christianity-on-the-shelf-following-spiritually-active-teen-years.

CHAPTER 1

Already Gone

Guard what has been entrusted to you, avoiding worldly and empty chatter and the opposing arguments of what is falsely called "knowledge" — which some have professed and thus gone astray from the faith. Grace be with you (1 Tim. 6:20–21).

I dare you. I dare you to try it this Sunday. Look to the right, and look to the left. While the pastor delivers his message, while the worship team sings their songs, while the youth pastor gives his announcements, look to the right and look to the left. Look at the children and look at the teens around you. Many of them will be familiar faces. They are the faces of your friends' sons and daughters. They are the friends that your children bring home after youth group. They are *your* children . . . the ones who have been faithfully following you to church for years.

Now, imagine that two-thirds of them have just disappeared.

That's right, *two-thirds* of them — the boys and the girls, the kids who are leaders of the school's Bible club, the kids who sit in the back row with their baseball caps pulled low over their eyes — imagine that two-thirds of them have just disappeared from your church.

Yes, look to the left and look to the right this Sunday. Put down your church bulletin; look at those kids and imagine that two-thirds of them aren't even there. Why?

Because they are *already gone.*

It's time to wake up and see the tidal wave washing away the foundation of your church. The numbers are in — and they don't look good. From across Christendom the reports are the same: *A mass exodus is underway. Most youth of today will not be coming to church tomorrow.* Nationwide polls and denominational reports are showing that the next generation is calling it quits on the traditional church. And it's not just happening on the nominal fringe; it's happening at the core of the faith.

Is that just a grim prediction? Is that just the latest arm-twisting from reactionary conservatives who are trying to instill fear into the parents and the teachers of the next generation? No, it's not just a prediction. It's a reality — as we will document clearly from commissioned professional and statistically valid research later in this book. In fact, it's already happening . . . just like it did in England; it's happening here in North America. *Now.* Like the black plagues that nearly wiped out the general population of Europe, a spiritual black plague has almost killed the next generation of European believers. A few churches are surviving. Even fewer are thriving. The vast majority are slowly dying. It's a spiritual epidemic, *really.* A wave of spiritual decay and death has almost entirely stripped a continent of its godly heritage, and now the same disease is infecting North America.

Many of us saw it coming but didn't want to admit it. After all, our churches looked healthy on the surface. We saw bubbling Sunday schools and dynamic youth ministries. As parents and grandparents we appreciatively graced the doors of the church, faithfully dragging our kids with us, as our ages pushed into the 40s and 50s and beyond. But a vacuum was forming: there were the college students who no longer showed up for the Sunday worship service, the newly married couple that never came back after the honeymoon. . . . Sure, there were exceptions and we were grateful for their dedication. For the most part, however, we saw that the 20- and 30-somethings from our congregations were increasingly AWOL. To be honest, none of us really wanted to admit it, did we? And so we began to justify to ourselves that maybe it wasn't happening at all.

Recent and irrefutable statistics are forcing us to face the truth. Respected pollster George Barna was one of the first to put numbers to the epidemic. Based on interviews with 22,000 adults and over 2,000 teenagers in 25 separate surveys, Barna unquestionably quantified the seriousness of the situation: *six out of ten 20-somethings who were involved in a church during their teen years are already gone.*[1] Despite strong levels of spiritual activity during the teen years, most 20-somethings disengage from active participation in the Christian faith during their young adult years — and often beyond that. Consider these findings:

- Nearly 50% of teens in the United States regularly attend church-related services or activities.

- More than three-quarters talk about their faith with their friends.

- Three out of five teens attend at least one youth group meeting at a church during a typical three-month period.

- One-third of teenagers participate in Christian clubs at school.[2]

That's all well and good, but do these numbers stand the test of time? Is the involvement of churched children and teens continuing into young adulthood? Unfortunately not. Not even close. The Barna

1. Barna Research Online, "Teenagers Embrace Religion but Are Not Excited About Christianity," January 10, 2000, www.Barna.org.
2. http://www.lifeway.com/lwc/article_main_page/0,1703,A%253D165951%2526 M%253D201117,00.html.

research is showing that religious activity in the teen years does not translate into spiritual commitment as individuals move into their 20s and 30s (and our own research, you are about to discover, will illuminate you with reasons as to why this occurs).

Most of them are pulling *away* from church, are spending *less* time alone studying their Bibles, are giving *very little* financially to Christian causes, are *ceasing* to volunteer for church activities, and are *turning their backs* on Christian media such as magazines, radio, and television. What does this look like numerically for today's 20-somethings?

- 61% of today's young adults who were regular church attendees are now "spiritually disengaged." They are not actively attending church, praying, or reading their Bibles.

- 20% of those who were spiritually active during high school are maintaining a similar level of commitment.

- 19% of teens were never reached by the Christian community, and they are still disconnected from the Church or any other Christian activities.

Shortly after Barna blew the whistle on the problem, individual denominations and churches began to take an honest look at what was happening as their children and teens began disappearing into the young adult years. Their findings confirmed the trends that Barna had found. Dozens of groups have looked at the issue from slightly different angles. Each study yields slightly different results, but their conclusions are unanimously startling. For example, when the Southern Baptist Convention researched the problem, they discovered that *more* than two-thirds of young adults who attended a Protestant church for at least a year in high school stopped attending for *at least* a year between the ages of 18 and 22.[3]

---

3. http://www.lifeway.com/lwc/article_main_page/0,1703,A%253D165951%2526 M%253D201117,00.html.

Twenty somethings struggle to stay active in Christian faith.

20% churched as teen, spiritually active at age 29

61% churched as teen, disengaged during twenties

19% never churched as teen, still unconnected

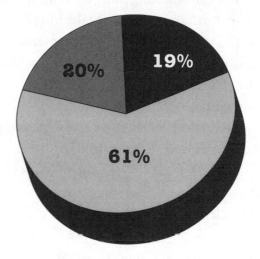

Source: The Barna Group, LTD 2006

There are exceptions, of course. Here and there we find a smattering of churches with vibrant participation from the 20-something age group. In some cities, we are seeing congregations develop that are made up almost exclusively of people from this age group. But unfortunately, these are the exceptions and not the rule. The trends that we are seeing can no longer be ignored. The epidemic is a reality. The abandoned church buildings of Europe are really just buildings, yet they are graphic symbols — warnings to those of us who are seeing the same trends in our local congregations: *we are one generation away from the evaporation of church as we know it.* Slowly but certainly the church of the future is headed toward the morgue and will continue to do so — unless we come to better understand what is happening and implement a clear, biblical plan to circumvent it.

The trends are known; more and more are finding out about them — but the vital question concerns what is the root problem of why this is happening. We need to know why if we are going to formulate possible solutions.

Who, Why, and What?

I began traveling and speaking in the United States in the 1980s. As an Australian, it didn't take long before I felt I had a good feeling for the pulse of American Christianity . . . and I saw some tremendous needs. At the time, America could rightly be labeled the greatest Christian nation on earth, the center of the economic world — and although the Church was equipped with nearly every conceivable tool and luxury for developing and expressing its faith — I could see that the Church was in great need.

Since moving to the United States in 1987, I have spoken in hundreds of different churches from many denominations, numerous Bible colleges, seminaries, and Christian conferences on American soil. I have talked with the pastors; I've listened to those in the congregations; I have experienced "worship" in almost every conceivable style and form. The ministry of Answers in Genesis is deeply committed to the American church. In fact, the faltering health of the Church in the greatest Christian nation on earth is what motivated my wife and me to move our family to this country in the first place. My wife and I testify that God called us as missionaries to America — particularly the American Church — to call it back to the authority of the Word of God beginning in Genesis.

The Bible calls the Church "the Body of Christ." Today, over 20 years after our move, the statistics prove that His body is bleeding profusely. The next generation of believers is draining from the churches, and it causes me great personal and professional concern. I've sat in the grand, but vacant, churches of Europe. I know where this is headed. Where Europe is today spiritually, America will be tomorrow — and for the same reasons, if the Church does not recognize where the foundational problem lies and address it.

When I began to seriously ponder Barna's numbers, naturally I wanted to find out more. For help, I called on a trusted and respected supporter of Answers in Genesis. As the chairman of America's Research Group, and as a leading marketing research and business analyst expert, Britt Beemer specializes in studying human behavior. Over the decades he has conducted dozens and dozens of surveys for leading corporations as well as small businesses. He analyzes the marketplace and the clientele, and makes recommendations that keep the companies excelling in a competitive world. When we were considering building the Creation Museum, we asked Britt if we could reasonably dream of 250,000 people visiting each year. Britt did his research and predicted that *400,000* people would visit the museum in the first year! He was wrong by two days. (The 400,000th visitor entered the museum 363 days after we opened.) Needless to say, when we had questions about the epidemic of people leaving church, we turned to him for answers.

Our goal was simple: We wanted to know *who* was leaving, *why* they were leaving, and *what* (if anything) could be done about it. To that end, Britt and his America's Research Group initiated a qualified study with probing questions to get powerful insight into the epidemic the Church is facing. To get to the core of the issues, his team studied *only* those whom we are most concerned about: every person in our sample said *they attended church every week or nearly every week when they were growing up, but never or seldom go today.*

We selected those between 20 and 30 who once attended conservative and "evangelical" churches. We wanted to look at the churches that claim to be Bible-believing congregations with Bible-preaching pastors. According to Barna, about 6 percent of people in their 20s and 30s can be considered "evangelical." This is about the same as the number of teenagers (5 percent).[4] The results from Britt's research would undoubtedly have been more drastic if we had considered more liberal congregations. We deliberately skewed the research toward conservatives so that we could all understand that whatever problems showed up would be much worse for the church population in general.

After 20,000 phone calls, with all the raw data in hand, Britt began to analyze the numbers. The things he discovered— as well as the things he *didn't* discover — began to shed light (in a quite astonishing way) on this monumental problem facing the future of Christianity.

---

4. www.barna.org.

The sample included:

1,000 individuals from coast to coast	balanced according to population and gender	with just over half being aged 25–29	with under half being aged 20–24

First of all, he *didn't* discover anything abnormal about the group as a whole. There weren't an unusual number of homeschoolers, or secular school kids, who were leaving. There wasn't a significant number of females compared to males that had decided to leave. In other words, the 60 percent plus of the evangelical kids who choose to leave the church look pretty much like the 40 percent who decide to stay — at least on the outside. The breakdown of those who left really fits the profile of the evangelical population in general.

So at first, the *who* question didn't seem to give us many answers. So then, *why?* Why did they leave the church? When we asked them this open-ended question, we got an earful.

At first, we were surprised (and a little disappointed) that there wasn't a single reason. It would have been nice to find a single identifiable virus somewhere. How simple it would have been to stereotype the whole group and point out one germ that had been causing the sickness to spread. But the numbers didn't say that. *A single identifiable culprit didn't appear.*

Other researchers have come to similar conclusions. When LifeWay did their research for the Southern Baptist Convention, 97 percent of the "dropouts" listed one or more specific life-change issues as a reason they left church. The most frequent reason they gave for leaving church was almost an indifferent shrug of the shoulders: "I

The top 10 reasons were:

1. 12% Boring service
2. 12% Legalism
3. 11% Hypocrisy of leaders
4. 10% Too political
5. 9% Self-righteous people
6. 7% Distance from home
7. 6% Not relevant to personal growth
8. 6% God would not condemn to hell
9. 5% Bible not relevant/not practical
10. 5% Couldn't find my preferred denomination in the area

simply wanted a break from church" (27 percent). The transition into college and adulthood also affected many: "I moved to college and stopped attending church" (25 percent), and "work responsibilities prevented me from attending" (23 percent). Others simply "moved too far away from the church to continue attending" (22 percent).[5] In all honesty, these kinds of results just seemed too shallow for us at Answers in Genesis. And they seemed too superficial to Britt as well. We have a massive epidemic on our hands, and researchers seemed to be content with answers that sounded like "I just didn't feel very good," or "I wasn't there because I chose to be someplace else." Too many researchers accept simple, superficial answers. They acknowledge that there is a massive shift taking place in the spiritual lives of young adults, but when it comes to really figuring out what's going on, they kind of throw up their hands and sigh, "I guess that's just the way it is!"

End of story? Not hardly. This is precisely why we teamed up with an expert like Britt Beemer who probes, and probes, and probes until he finds the right reasons. We found the real reasons, though some of them will shake many churches to their very core.

Never content with the easy answers that people give to justify their behavior, Britt is an expert in consumer behavior who taps into their minds as he finds out what people really believe in order to reveal what is driving their behavior. Until Answers in Genesis commissioned this study, never before had this type of research been conducted — and our research was formulated to not just deeply probe what people believe but answer the questions in regard to WHY people believe what they do. We can now identify the real answers as well as the causes affecting young people who leave the church.

As Britt studied his data, it was obvious that multiple issues are behind the exodus from church. The *why?* question would prove to be more complicated than many expected. But soon, as the numbers became more clear, patterns emerged, assumptions were destroyed,

---

5. http://www.lifeway.com/lwc/article_main_page/0,1703,A%253D165951%2526 M%253D201117,00.html.

and quirky findings surfaced. One of the most important and startling findings turned out not to answer the *why?* question, but rather the *when?* question.

Of these thousand 20 to 29-year-old evangelicals who attended church regularly but no longer do so:

95% of them attended church regularly during their elementary and middle school years	55% attended church regularly during high school	Of the thousand, only 11% were still going to church during their early college years

I think this is one of the most revealing and yet challenging statistics in the entire survey — and something we didn't expect. Most people assume that students are lost in college. We've always been trying to prepare our kids for college (and I still think that's a critical thing to do, of course), but it turns out that only 11 percent of those who have left the Church were still attending during the college years. Almost 90 percent of them were lost in middle school and high school. By the time they got to college they were already gone! About 40 percent are leaving the Church during elementary and middle school years! Most people assumed that elementary and middle school is a fairly neutral environment where children toe the line and follow in the footsteps of their parents' spirituality. Not so. I believe that over half of these kids were lost before we got them into high school! Whatever diseases are fueling the epidemic of losing our young people, they are infecting our students much, much earlier than most assumed. Let me say this again:

We are losing many more people by middle school and many more by high school than we will ever lose in college.

Many parents will fork out big bucks to send these students to Christian colleges, hoping to protect them in their faith. But the fact is, they're already gone. They were lost while still in the fold. They were disengaging while they were still sitting in the pews. They were preparing their exit while they were faithfully attending youth groups and Sunday schools.

What a reminder to parents (and Christian leaders) to do exactly what God's Word instructs us to do — to "train up a child in the way he should go . . ." (Prov. 22:6). And further, "These words which I command you today shall be in your heart. You shall teach them diligently to your children, and shall talk of them when you sit in your house, when you walk by the way, when you lie down, and when you rise up" (Deut. 6:6–7; NKJV). What a reminder to teach children from when they are born — and a reminder to be diligent in providing the right sort of training/curricula, etc., for children.

Sadly, I think many see children's programs as entertainment, teaching Bible stories, and so on, but when they get older we need to think about preparing them somehow for college — but as our research showed, by then they are already gone! For most, it was basically too late!

This topic regarding when we begin to lose our kids is where the study began to get very interesting and very illuminating. For example:

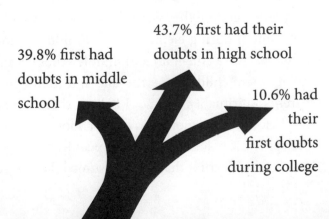

Those who no longer believe that all of the accounts and stories in the Bible are true:

39.8% first had doubts in middle school

43.7% first had their doubts in high school

10.6% had their first doubts during college

Clearly, there is a slightly delayed reaction going on. The doubts come first, followed shortly by departure. Students didn't begin doubting *in* college, they simply departed *by* college. Again, if you look around in your church today, two-thirds of those who are sitting among us have already left in their hearts, it will only take a couple years before their bodies are absent as well.

The Beemer study has a tremendous amount to offer the churches, the pastors, the parents, and the researchers who are sincerely looking into this problem. Britt's study didn't look just at behavior; he looked at belief. By making correlations between those beliefs and the behavior and intentions of those who have left the Church, the veil was lifted, powerful new insights were revealed, and very surprising results were illuminated. In the pages ahead we will give you the highlights of some of these numbers. But brace yourself, because in many instances the results are shocking, and they point a finger at many well-intentioned, firmly established programs and traditions of churches that are utterly failing the children who faithfully attend every Sunday morning.

You will need to swallow hard and be prepared to consider things very carefully; Be ready to give up long-held, cherished notions in regard to certain church programs of which perhaps you would never have considered the slightest possibility that there was such a serious problem as this research clearly showed.

First, we will investigate key aspects of the epidemic, including:

- the effects of Sunday school

- the two different kinds of kids who are leaving the Church and why it's so important to know the difference

- why the Church has lost its value and is now considered irrelevant

Second, we will investigate the solutions that are within our grasp:

- how to defend the Christian faith and uphold the authority of the Bible from the very first verse

- what it means (and doesn't mean) to live by the Bible

- the revolution that is reclaiming "church" in this culture

Along the way the investigation will be spiced up with a variety of fascinating findings regarding the following:

- music

- friends

- unbiblical church traditions

- teaching

- beliefs about Genesis

If you are a parent, a pastor, or a Christian educator, then this re-search is for you. Or maybe you are one of the millions of students who are thinking about leaving the Church or have already done so. If so, I challenge you to let the numbers speak for themselves and then be ready to allow God to use you in new ways to make a difference for the sake of the next generation and the Church. Even though the results were obtained in America, because it has had the greatest Christian influence in the world and has been an enormous influence on the world (Christian literature, missionaries, etc.), it is likely that such re-search would show similar (at best) or much worse results in other countries.

Yes, I challenge you. This Sunday, look to the left and then look to the right. According to our research, two-thirds of the children and teens you see will be gone in a matter of years. *What* can be done about it? Plenty, as you will soon see!

Britt's Bit: The AIG-ARG Connection

On behalf of Ken Ham, I want to thank you for picking up this book. I make my living generating numbers and statistics, and they are an important part of my personal ministry. When numbers and statistics are interpreted correctly they mean something. They aren't just arbitrary measurements for things that don't matter. Numbers do matter. They represent things that are real, that are measurable, that can be observed, and (in many cases) that can be changed with the right remedies. That's what America's Research Group is all about. At ARG we draw conclusions that are meaningful to our clients. We are behavioral scientists who study human behavior. ARG provides each client a foundation built on practical, useful information that ensures their ongoing success.

That's why I am such a firm believer in Answers in Genesis. Not only is their ministry important, but AIG is a reminder of what God can do through one person who steps out in faith and allows God to use them to defend and proclaim the truth. Ken moved his family to the United States more than 20 years ago, having started a ministry out of the trunk of his car and a few cardboard boxes in his house. I don't think anyone would have believed (particularly Ken) what God had in store for a ministry of such humble beginnings.

Today, the Answers in Genesis website gets *millions of visitors per year*. Tens of thousands of resources (books, DVDs, curricula, magazines, etc.) move through AIG's warehouse year after year. A small army of trained speakers are reaching tens of thousands of people face-to-face on every continent on the globe except Antarctica. (As far as I know, no one has volunteered to go there quite yet!)

I love keeping track of the AIG ministry and what people say about it. I've been tracking public opinion religiously (pun intended), and I have a deep desire to protect and to equip this ministry. When the Creation Museum opened, it created a national media tsunami, and at least one-third of the comments voiced about the ministry were clearly negative. The naysayers had their day, but they didn't last. Today, only 1/20th of the comments about the museum are negative. I think that is an amazing accomplishment. As I projected, 400,000 people came through those doors in the first year.

I make my living studying human behavior and attitudes statistically, which gives me a unique viewpoint of how and why people act the way they do. I sincerely invite you to come along with my friend and ministry cohort Ken Ham as he takes you on a personal tour through my numbers. I'll be throwing in my "bit" on a regular basis, giving you my take on the statistics and their importance. As you begin to understand the trends of the past, and see where the Church is at present, you will discover highly practical action points that will make a difference in the future. I believe that if you get a handle on a few of the numbers that describe what is happening in the Church today, you will see the potential for change that resides within you as a pastor, a parent, or a Christian educator. And that's important. The next generation is counting on us.

CHAPTER 2

Sunday School Syndrome

Everything I know I Learned in Kindergarten — title of a best-selling book for adults.

This Sunday morning a familiar scene will play itself out at churches from coast to coast. Minivans and SUVs will open like pop cans in the parking lots of various denominations, spewing forth their contents of kids. With Bibles in one hand and car-seats in the other, parents will herd their excited children toward the doors. In the hallways, the kids will split up by age and be welcomed into classrooms full of laughter and life and hope. Teachers will embrace these kids as if they are their own for about 45 minutes. They will pour their hearts and souls into the children and teens with the help of videos, various curricula resources, Bible stories, crayons, crackers, CD music, computer graphics, flannel graphs, white boards, cookies, cotton balls, popsicle sticks, prayers, and pipe cleaners. . . . It all looks so safe and so healthy — an inseparable part of the fabric of spiritual life in the western world.

"Did you often attend Sunday school?"

yes. 61%   **no.** 39%

In our survey of 1,000 20-somethings who regularly attended church as children and teens, we asked the question, "Did you often attend Sunday school?" In reply, 61 percent said yes; 39 percent said no. That's about what you would expect, isn't it? After all, not everyone is committed enough to make the effort to get to Sunday school, right? Only those who are more concerned about the spiritual and moral health of their kids, right? Because we all assume that Sunday school is good for them, correct? The ritual of Sunday school is so interwoven into American church life that it's hardly worth mentioning, right? Wrong. Our research uncovered something very disturbing:

> Sunday school is actually more likely to be detrimental to the spiritual and moral health of our children.

Now before you react to this, please hear us out and consider the research — real research that is statistically valid and gives us a true look at what is going on.

Compared to the 39 percent who do *not* go to Sunday school, contrary to what many of you may believe, the research showed that students who *regularly* attend Sunday school are actually:

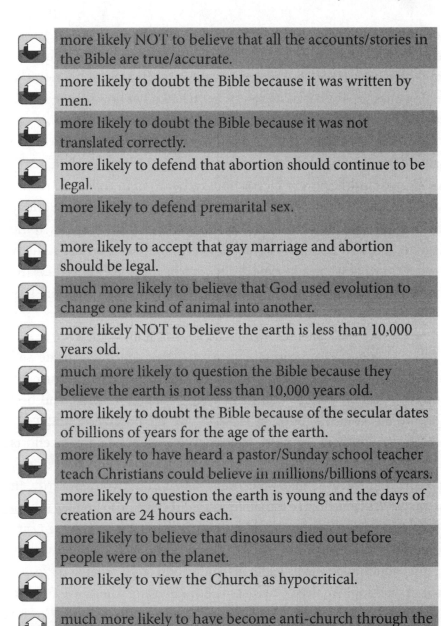

- more likely NOT to believe that all the accounts/stories in the Bible are true/accurate.

- more likely to doubt the Bible because it was written by men.

- more likely to doubt the Bible because it was not translated correctly.

- more likely to defend that abortion should continue to be legal.

- more likely to defend premarital sex.

- more likely to accept that gay marriage and abortion should be legal.

- much more likely to believe that God used evolution to change one kind of animal into another.

- more likely NOT to believe the earth is less than 10,000 years old.

- much more likely to question the Bible because they believe the earth is not less than 10,000 years old.

- more likely to doubt the Bible because of the secular dates of billions of years for the age of the earth.

- more likely to have heard a pastor/Sunday school teacher teach Christians could believe in millions/billions of years.

- more likely to question the earth is young and the days of creation are 24 hours each.

- more likely to believe that dinosaurs died out before people were on the planet.

- more likely to view the Church as hypocritical.

- much more likely to have become anti-church through the years.

- more likely to believe that good people don't need to go to church.

Read that list again. No, we don't have it backward. Yes, you're reading it correctly. These results are extremely alarming — in fact, quite shocking. (I had to look at it several times before I could believe it.) They are so contrary to what we would have assumed that they should feel like a rude slap in the face. And remember, these findings were the result of probing questions by a leading researcher who knows how to gather data and statistically analyze it to give us a true picture of the situation.

This was our most stunning and disconcerting result of the entire survey. First, we found out that we were losing our kids in elementary school, middle school, and high school rather than in college. Then we found out that Sunday school is one of the reasons why. The "Sunday school syndrome" is contributing to the epidemic, rather than helping alleviate it. These numbers are statistically significant and absolutely contrary to what we would expect. This is a brutal wake-up call for the Church, showing how our programs and our approaches to Christian education are failing dismally.

Before we investigate this further, however, I want to say a few words to those of you who are committed to Christian education inside and outside of the church. My hat goes off to you. I thank you. I sincerely commend you for taking action and giving your time, skills, and best efforts to invest in the future generation. We are not questioning your dedication, intentions, or passion. In fact, we believe that your efforts are far too often taken for granted and never thanked enough. We don't question your integrity and we certainly don't doubt your sincerity. In our survey, less than half of the students said they came to Sunday school to see their friends. That means that *you* were their contact point. *You* are the ones who are sincerely trying to build a bridge for them into a healthy spiritual adulthood. The problem is that, by and large, what you are do-ing isn't working. We need to ask some hard questions here. We need to be willing to swallow our pride, if necessary, as we find the answers. And we will offer solutions — real solutions — if the Church will take these findings to heart and be prepared to face the challenge head-on.

Disturbing Details

Three out of five individuals in our survey said they "often attended Sunday school." Of those who attended Sunday school, over seven in ten *said* Sunday school lessons were "helpful." Our results, however, disproved that perception.

In many situations, Sunday school didn't necessarily hurt, but it certainly didn't help. When asked, "Does the Bible contain errors?" sadly, Sunday school made no difference. (About 39 percent of each group said yes to this question.) When asked, "Do you believe you are saved and will go to heaven upon death?" there was almost no statistical difference — which really is very disconcerting. In most of the categories, there was such a slight difference between the "yes" or "no" answers of these two groups that the "I don't know" answers became a big factor. The results show that Sunday school is actually having an overall *negative* impact on beliefs, even though these differences were often quite slight in a number of instances. *The obvious conclusion is that Sunday school really had no impact on what children believed in these critical areas.*

For example, when asked if they believed in the creation of Adam in the Garden of Eden, Sunday school had no significant effect on the answers. The same can be said for the story of Sodom and Gomorrah and Lot's wife. The same can be said of Noah's ark and the global Flood. Belief in the Tower of Babel was nearly identical. In these areas Sunday school did nothing — it wasn't a help or a detriment. The numbers indicate that Sunday school actually didn't do *anything* to help them develop a Christian worldview. In several other areas, as shocking as this sounds, the reality we have to face is that Sunday school clearly harmed the spiritual growth of the kids. Consider these questions:

"Do you believe that God used evolution to create human beings?"

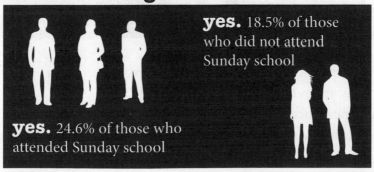

yes. 18.5% of those who did not attend Sunday school

yes. 24.6% of those who attended Sunday school

"Do you believe that God used evolution to change one kind of animal into another?"

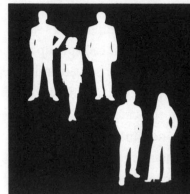

yes. 27.2% of Sunday school attenders

yes. 18.8% of those who did not go to Sunday school believed in this type of evolution

Toward the end of this chapter, we will give you an explanation as to why we believe such a situation exists.

It's safe to say that Sunday school attendance is tied to higher percentages of belief in evolution. The same can be said about important moral issues.

"Do you believe that premarital sex is wrong?"

47.7% of students who did not attend Sunday school believe that premarital sex is wrong

40.8% of Sunday school attenders believe that premarital sex is wrong

And what about the main issue we are concerned about in this book? Why are our kids leaving the Church?

These next three findings may shock you because you would naturally feel those who attended Sunday school would have deeper religious convictions. However, we found the exact opposite.

"Do you feel good people don't need to go to church?"

yes. 39.3% of Sunday school attenders

yes. interestingly, only 28.9% of non-attenders

"Do you feel the Church is relevant to your needs today?"

no. Only 39.6% of those who did not attend Sunday school felt like church is not relevant to their needs today.

no. 46.4% of Sunday school attenders

"Do you believe that you have become anti-church through the years?"

yes. 39.1% of those who attended Sunday school

yes. 26.9% of those who didn't go to Sunday school

This should cause us to gasp. When compared to those who never went to Sunday school, more Sunday school attenders believe that good people don't need to go to church, more feel like the church is less relevant, and more have become increasingly anti-church over the years.

The brutal conclusion is that, on the whole, the Sunday school programs of today are statistical failures.

Ouch!

I know that's going to hurt many of you who are devoted and dedicated to these programs — as well as those of you who are depending on these programs to properly influence your children. I'm sure various Sunday school curricula publishers will want to become defensive about their resources. But listen, if you are depending on these programs to properly teach and influence your children, it is just not happening.

Out of the 1,000 interviews, 606 were former Sunday school students, and the Church failed these people miserably. As children and teenagers they were there almost every Sunday; they were committed and they were present; they heard the lessons and they nodded their heads . . . and it had a nominal and even negative effect on their faith.

If I were a church leader, I would first sit down and cry and pour my heart out to the Lord. And rightly so. I would then find a new Sunday school curriculum that better prepares young people to maintain their faith. These numbers would be telling me that I need to earnestly look at some radical changes, and I would be working hard toward doing what is needed to reverse this situation.

Taught but Not Caught

All of these numbers would be a little bit easier to accept if we had surveyed a broader cross-section of Christian churches. If these numbers included all of the nominal, liberal churches (particularly those that don't even claim to stand on the Word of God), then these results would be a little bit more understandable. But they don't. Remember what we said at the beginning about the type of person we identified for this survey. These results have come from the Christian education programs of the most dedicated, Scripture-affirming churches out there — imagine what the situation must be in the Church as a whole!

Is it a problem of not being taught? Considering these people came from conservative church backgrounds, consider these numbers from our research:

- Of those who attended Sunday school, over 9 in 10 said that their Sunday school classes taught them that the Bible was true and accurate.

- Only 1 in 10 said their pastor/Sunday school teacher taught that Christians could believe in Darwinian evolution.

- One in 4 said their pastors and Sunday school teachers taught that Christians could believe in an earth that is millions or billions of years old.

- Over 4 in 5 said their pastor or Sunday school teacher taught that God created the earth in six 24-hour days.

- Only 1 in 16 said their pastors or Sunday school teachers taught that the Book of Genesis was a myth or legend and not real history.

Actually, as we will explain later on, there is a major problem with *how* they were taught. These people who went to conservative churches heard many of the right things for the most part (though the situation would be much less so on the whole), but did they "hear" in a way that

Further,

- 2/5 said the Bible contains errors.
- Less than 2/5 said they believe all the accounts and stories in the Bible are true and accurate.

equipped them to believe in their hearts what the Bible clearly stated, and were they equipped to be able to defend this teaching in the real world they live in?

Clearly, we do have a problem on our hands. The causes for the problems are many, but one thing is for sure: Sunday school isn't solving it. High school is when we lost nearly half of this group; a big group was lost even earlier in middle school due to doubt in the accounts and stories in the Bible being true. Of those who don't believe all the accounts and stories in the Bible are true and accurate, four in nine said they had their first doubts in high school.

As the astronaut exclaimed, "Houston, we have a problem!" We will look at our "problem" in great detail in the chapters ahead. Several major concerns will become evident: the concern over biblical authority, the history behind our descent into this abyss, and the great disconnect this has caused when people try to make a connection between their spirituality and reality. What are we going to do?

You will see later in the book that much can (and must!) be done. Great debate is raging right now about the future of Christian education programs. What are some of the ideas?

1. Should we eradicate?

This is a very extreme suggestion, but since we have an extreme epidemic on our hands, it needs to be at least discussed. A growing number of people within the evangelical church are suggesting that we do away with children's and youth ministries altogether. Consider these thoughts from the Reformed Baptist Church blog site *The World from My Window*[1]:

> It seems as if we are always trying to fix what is broken with youth ministry. Has it crossed anyone else's mind that maybe youth ministry shouldn't be fixed because youth ministry **IS** a major part of the problem?!

1. http://theworldfrommywindow.blogspot.com/2006/09/barna-confirms-teens-are-leaving.html.

. . . Just in case you were wondering. I am not anti-youth or anti-youth pastor. My two brothers function in the role of youth pastors (including the famous Ken Fields). I was a youth pastor for six years and I am greatly concerned with the future of our younger generations.

Is that idea too radical? Could it possibly be an improvement to get rid of Sunday school and youth ministries altogether? That almost sounds blasphemous. After all, aren't our concepts of "church" and "Sunday school" inseparable? Not necessarily. Just because our generation has always done it that way doesn't mean that we have to continue to do it that way. George Barna and Frank Viola note that Sunday school isn't even historical:

> The Sunday school is also a relatively recent invention, born some 1,700 years after Christ. A newspaper publisher named Robert Raikes (1736–1811) from Britain is credited with being its founder. In 1780, Raikes established a school in "Scout Alley" for poor children. Raikes did not begin the Sunday school for the purpose of religious instruction. Instead, he founded it to teach poor children the basics of education. . . . The Sunday school took off like wildfire, spreading to Baptist, Congregational, and Methodist churches throughout England.[2]

Part of the concern is that the mere existence of youth ministry and Sunday school allows parents to shrug off their responsibilities as the primary teachers, mentors, and pastors to their family. The other part of the concern is that, again, what we are doing just isn't working. If the existence of our Christian education programs in their current forms are certainly not helping — and in some situations even doing harm — why not dump them altogether?

---

2. George Barna and Frank Viola, *Pagan Christianity?* (Carol Stream, IL: Barna-Books, 2007), p. 212.

However, we are not advocating eradication! We want to be solution-oriented, as you will see, so that we can effectively reach these young people with the truth of God's Word.

2. Renovate

This recommendation isn't quite so extreme — and it is one we recommend. Our children need more training, more nurturing, more teaching than ever — but we need to turn things around so Sunday school isn't doing the opposite.

We believe it's possible that the current Christian education programs within the Church don't need to be eradicated, but they certainly need to be renovated. Churches need to appraise the teachers teaching Sunday School and ensure they know how to answer the skeptical questions and know how to teach apologetics — and know how to teach the age group being entrusted to them. It's one thing to tell students what to believe, it's another thing to teach and communicate that in a convincing and gripping way.

Churches need to totally reevaluate the curricula they use (including their VBS programs), and at the very least supplement at all age levels and all years with good apologetics curricula. And we are not just talking about creation apologetics — we mean general biblical apologetics as well. Most church-going adults cannot adequately defend the basics of their Christian faith or basic doctrines, let alone defend the faith against the skeptical questions of this scientific age. How many can really even properly answer questions such as: Where did the Bible come from? What does it mean to have faith? What does it mean that the Bible is inspired? Aren't there other books that some say should be in the Bible? How do you know Jesus is God? — just to name a few. More and more curricula (such as VBS programs and supplemental curricula for different ages) that is apologetic in nature is being produced to begin to fulfill the above need. Some resources are described in the bibliography.

When we talk of "renovating," we mean something much more aggressive than simply "redecorating." A little updating isn't going to do the job. The entire structure and focus of our programs need to be reconsidered; we need to be willing to make radical changes in the format and the style of these programs to determine how they can be most effective in teaching truth to our children and overcoming the issues that are undermining biblical authority in their thinking and driving them away from the Church.

Let's be honest. Our entire culture (including secular schools) is aggressively teaching the apologetics of evolution and secular humanism. They teach our students how to defend a humanistic worldview, and they model that worldview. They show all the reasons that what they are teaching is supposedly true. The secularists are teaching our children how to defend the secular faith, and connecting it to the real world — and here we are in churches teaching wonderful Bible stories and reinforcing in their minds that they can believe the secularists and that the Bible is not really connected to the real world. No wonder we are losing them. (See the section for the Christian educator in chapter 7 which deals with solid curriculum for more details on the problems with Sunday school lessons.)

Unless the facts behind the Christian faith are clearly and convincingly communicated in a way that students can learn and remember, their faith will not stand the assault of doubt from the world. It's not enough to just tell students, "Believe in Jesus!" Faith that is not founded on fact will ultimately falter in the storm of secularism that our students face every day.

In many cases, when we look at what is being taught in the Sunday schools, we're just teaching on an inspirational or a moral level. The Sunday sermon usually dishes out more of the same. Neither one is providing the necessary support and education students need. In many cases, they are getting two lessons on a Sunday, and neither are really relevant to them. It's not just the Sunday school, it's the sermon, the VBS, it's most of the teaching programs — they are not helping them in this postmodern culture where it is becoming the norm to attack and marginalize Christians. They are not coping — they are not able to cope — they haven't been trained to cope.

Perhaps you agree with us that it's going too far to eradicate, but hopefully you will agree it's certainly time to renovate. Radical renovation is needed urgently. We are losing the next generation — we are losing the culture.

3. Don't delegate

Listen carefully. We're certainly not saying that Sunday school *can't* be effective in teaching the truth about God's Word. We're just saying that in its current form it *isn't*. If nothing else, a parent should look at these data and feel a rush of sober realization. If you, as a parent, have been putting the responsibility for the religious education of your child on your church's Sunday school, you need to realize that the statistics say the job isn't getting done. As we have seen, in many cases and for many different reasons, it's not helping, it's hurting. So this coming Sunday, don't feel like you have absolved yourself of responsibility when you drop your child at Sunday school. This is your job. Do not totally delegate it to someone else — as, sadly, many parents seem to do.

Deuteronomy 6:4–10 and Ephesians 6:1–4 clearly exhort parents to teach, disciple, and train their own children. Regardless of what's happening in the Sunday school youth groups, pulpit, and Bible studies of your church, the responsibility for ministry to our kids has never been removed from the parents. It's time to pick that ball up again and jump in the game. James H. Rutz, in his thought-provoking book *The Open Church: How to Bring Back the Exciting Life of the First Century Church,* has the heart and the courage to take an honest look at the Sunday school ritual and test its effectiveness:

> Take Sunday school for example. God's plan for religious education is Dad. It's a 4,000-year-old plan that's worked like a watch since the days of Abraham. But if your weekly gathering doesn't equip Dad to open his mouth at home and be a teacher of the Word — well, Sunday school is your next best bet. (Programming Dad would be easier.)[3]

---

3. James H. Rutz, *The Open Church: How to Bring Back the Exciting Life of the First Century Church* (Auburn, ME: SeedSowers, 1992), p. 19.

I understand what this author is saying, but we would say it is actually a 6,000-year-old plan, going back to the first dad, Adam.

If your parents shirked their responsibility for training you spiritually, you will need to break the chain of biblical illiteracy and spiritual irresponsibility in your family tree. If your church hasn't been stepping up to the plate to equip you, I would suggest a book I wrote with my brother Stephen, *Raising Godly Children in an Ungodly World — Leaving a Lasting Legacy*.[4] Steve and I had a great blessing of being raised by a father (and mother) who took creative and determined responsibility for teaching their kids from God's Word, and living a biblical life. Our father, as the spiritual head of the house, stood uncompromisingly on the Word of God, determined to be equipped to answer the skeptical questions of the age, setting an example for his children that prepared us for the ministries we are involved in today. We would gratefully pass on to you what he passed on to us so that you can pass it on to your kids. Again, don't delegate this. It's one of the most rewarding and important aspects of being a parent. And do it right now. There's no time to waste.

What is interesting to me is that a person who has not heard of the research being reported in this book, and who has never heard me speak on this topic, wrote to my brother Stephen after reading the book referred to above and said:

> "I read your book *Raising Godly Children in an Ungodly World*. . . . I thoroughly enjoyed it and felt greatly challenged as a Sunday school teacher. I just realized how many people went through Sunday school in Australia and came out of it, and never come back to church again. It makes me reevaluate the role that I played at our Sunday school, whether I am playing my part right, drawing children to know God or pushing them away from God without even knowing it. Your book came in just as a wake up call!"

4. Ken Ham and Steve Ham, *Raising Godly Children in an Ungodly World* (Green Forest, AR: Master Books, 2008).

Not a Simple Epidemic

This Sunday, the ritual of Sunday school and teen ministry will again repeat itself. Through the data collected by Britt Beemer in this survey, we now know how typical Sunday school programs have affected our children. The Sunday school syndrome is a serious contributor to the overall problem of students exiting the Church. A true and urgent commitment to address the problem is probably more important than the specific solutions that are eventually implemented. Again, when 60 percent of our kids are leaving the Church, there will be no single solution to the overall problem — there is no single inoculation that will make us immune. The truth of the matter is that the epidemic affects each of us as individuals, because each of us is part of the greater Body of Christ. Together, working as a body, a multifaceted response to the disease can materialize. Lord willing, the mass exodus can be slowed, if not reversed, and be transformed into something new and more powerful than the typical, traditional forms we are now using.

Imagine if we started (in our homes and churches) raising generations of children who stood uncompromisingly on the Word of God, knew how to defend the Christian faith, could answer the skeptical questions of this age, and had a fervor to share the gospel from the authority of God's Word with whomever they met! This could change the world.

In the next chapter, we will look deeper into the lives of those who are leaving the Church. What the numbers taught us about them will be essential as you move into the future and discern what *you* can do to address this problem. Let there be no mistake, it's time to do something — it's time for *you* to do something. If not, you might as well sleep in this Sunday. The statistics show that not going won't hurt your kids one bit. In fact, they might be better for it.

Britt's Bit: Not by Chance

You have to be careful with numbers. People often say, "You can prove anything you want to with statistics," and they are partially right.

As a consumer researcher, I've seen people use every trick in the book to try to prove their point no matter whether the data supported it or not.

For example, what if a politician told you that "70 percent of students in the country scored above the national average"? Would you believe him? Could you believe him? No way. The law of averages says that half the country will be above average. (The other half, of course, will be below average.)

A news anchor recently said, "Over half of Americans approve of abortion." The truth is, only 38 percent approve of abortion, but 13 percent are still undecided. So by adding the undecideds with those who oppose it, they conclude that 50 percent accept it. A few years ago I was hired to conduct a study of 1,000 consumers across America. When we finished the survey we realized that we had omitted a question that the client really wanted. So, at our expense, we interviewed another 1,000 consumers with the original questions, plus the one new one. Amazingly, when I reviewed all the data from the two different surveys conducted within a week of each other, no answer varied more than 1.8 percent, well within the 3.8 plus or minus statistical error factor.

In this study, when we say that there is a difference between two numbers, we can prove that mathematically. When you hear statistics from other people, you'll just have to be careful and double check to make sure that they aren't twisting or fabricating what they are saying!

CHAPTER 3

Not What You'd Expect

God sees not as man sees, for man looks at the outward appearance, but the LORD looks at the heart (1 Sam. 16:7).

This Sunday, William and his family are going to sleep in. Across the street, Karen and her husband are going to do the same. The day will look much the same for each of them: breakfast in pajamas, the Sunday comics, a few chores around the house, an afternoon filled with some sort of an outing, movie, or a visit with family and friends.

On the outside, their lives look about the same — typical middle-class suburbanites, living out their days in the midst of the nine to five. Yes, Karen and William have a lot in common, but they also share something that isn't quite so obvious: Karen and William are former church kids. Two names out of the thousand that we surveyed. Perhaps they represent your neighbor next door, perhaps they are your siblings . . . perhaps they are *your* kids. Karen and William spent the better part of two decades in church on Sunday mornings. No more. They are already gone.

When dinnertime rolls around, however, we see something is drastically different about them. Before the meal is served, William and his family join hands and give sincere thanks for God's provision. Karen and her husband talk about current events in the news and the week ahead. When the dishes are done and the kids are tucked in, William will plop down on his bed and read the Bible he keeps on his nightstand. As the living words of Scripture resonate in his soul he senses the familiar and calming presence of the Holy Spirit in his heart. He dozes off in sincere prayer, asking for God's guidance and grace for the days ahead. "Maybe next Sunday . . . ," he thinks. "Yeah, maybe next week I'll go back." Karen and her husband, on the other hand, will catch a re-run on the television, make a few plans for the upcoming week, and turn off the light. If they think about God at all, the thoughts are skeptical. And going back to church never even crosses their mind.

Monday morning, William and Karen will wave to each other as they pull out of their driveways and head back to their jobs. Yes, on the surface they appear to be very similar people. But they're not . . . and that's not what we would expect.

The Dividing Line

When we commissioned Britt Beemer to study the kids who are leaving church, we knew that we could not be satisfied with superficial answers. We wanted to know *who, why,* and *what.* If there were simple answers to those questions, someone would have certainly found them by now (and would have become famous by applying the one-size-fits-all solution that would have solved the problem once and for all). Of course, that's not the case. Epidemics are never simple. There are root causes. There are things that cause them to accelerate. There are things that can be done to curb them from spreading. There are things that can be done to help those who are already sick get well.

Britt's data, as we expected, went deep. Rather than being satisfied with obvious observations that profile people like William and Karen, Britt went for the heart. And what he found proved to be profoundly descriptive and yet very simple and practical.

Central to this study was the issue of belief. You simply cannot explain the behavior without understanding the beliefs behind the behaviors. "Belief" is invisible. The only way to see it is through actions — yet the same actions might be the result of different beliefs. Remember that everyone in our sample of 1,000 grew up regularly going to church but seldom or never go today. Britt asked several questions to determine whether biblical belief was at the root of the exodus from the Church.

This was one of several "watershed questions" of the survey because those who accepted all the accounts and stories in the Bible had a much different viewpoint throughout all the questions in the survey. These questions and the results revealed in the survey helped us discern when these people's belief in the accuracy of Scripture began to be eroded in their thinking.

"Do you believe all the accounts/stories in the Bible are true/accurate?"

a full 38% of people who left the church answered yes

44% said no

18% didn't know

So it could also be said that a full 62 percent of the sample did not believe all the accounts and stories in the Bible. Affirming our earlier conclusions, most of those who do not believe in the full accuracy of the Bible began to doubt in elementary, middle, and high school (88 percent), while only 11 percent began to doubt in college.

You might think their belief systems were alike, but when Britt started asking further questions, it was clear that they were flowing in one of two different directions. We seemed to be dealing with two groups of people when it came to belief: those who believe the Bible and those who harbor serious doubts about the Scriptures.

We asked numerous questions about the Bible. Some of them related to evolution and the age of the earth, others questioned belief in specific historical biblical events. In our opinion, *88 percent of the people in the survey incorrectly answered at least one of these questions,* particularly questions dealing with the age of the earth.

But 12 percent of those surveyed answered all the questions correctly. So why did those 12 percent leave? They all went to church growing up. They still claim to believe the major tenets of the Christian faith . . . but there they are on our AWOL list. Clearly, factors other than their belief in the Bible and traditional Christian values have influenced their decision to leave. As we crunched the data from our survey, it became apparent that commonly held stereotypes of those who are leaving the Church are not altogether accurate. Church attendees tend to blame the epidemic on those who have left. We label them as apostate, insincere, uncommitted, lazy, or indifferent. You can believe that the Bible is true and intellectually accepted but still not feel called to go to church on Sunday. As we studied the research findings further, we soon found we were dealing with two different types of individuals who were no longer attending church: *those who come at least during Easter and/ or Christmas — and those who don't come at all.*

If you are a regular church attendee, these numbers will not be surprising to you. Christmas and Easter are definitely the big days at church. The irregular regular attendees almost always show up and you see this flood of new faces. They are not a regular part of the congregation yet have come to celebrate and remember the birth and Resurrection of Jesus Christ nonetheless — and they are probably parking in *your* spot and sitting in *your seats*. You might be surprised to be sitting next to one of those 20 year olds during a Christmas or Easter service.

"Do you attend church services at Easter or Christmas?"

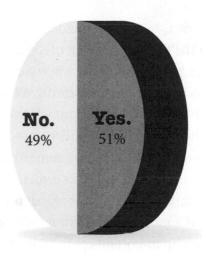

No.
49%

Yes.
51%

And then there were those who never come to church, not even at Easter or Christmas. Over 30 percent of those who never go to church also say that they "don't think of it at all." For them, church is out of sight and out of mind. (These guys are *really* already gone.)

What is one of the core issues that predict that someone will go to church to celebrate the Christian holidays as opposed to staying home? It appears that belief has a lot to do with it.

	Attend on holidays	**Never attend**
Do you believe all the books of the Bible are inspired by God?	72.8% said yes	50.2% said yes
Do you believe in creation as stated in the Bible?	87.2 % said yes	55.9% said yes
Do you believe in the creation of Adam and Eve in the Garden of Eden?	91.3% said yes	50.6% said yes
Do you believe all the accounts/stories in the Bible are true/accurate?	52.4% said yes	23.8% said yes
Do you believe you are saved and will go to heaven upon death?	72.2% said yes	58.7% said yes

In fact, when we asked them if secular science caused them to doubt the Bible, 56 percent of those who never attend said yes. A much smaller portion of those who worship on Christmas and Easter said yes (36.8 percent). Significantly, 44 percent of those who never attend church believe in evolution; while only 12 percent of those who visit on holidays believe the molecules to man theory.

Of those who don't ever come to church, 24 percent of those who believe that the Bible contains errors pointed to Genesis. Compare that to the group that still comes to worship at Christmas and Easter and we find out that a much smaller group falls in that category. Genesis issues are certainly an important contributing factor. Surprisingly, a full 50 percent of the people who do not go to church at all still believe in the creation of Adam and Eve, so there are obviously other issues that collectively are keeping them from church. Many of them believe in the Genesis accounts (though what many mean by this might not be a young-earth perspective), but they still don't go to church for other reasons.

The data support the idea that those who go at Christmas and Easter are still genuine believers who want to have a group worship experience and celebrate the most important events in Christianity. The non-attendees are much more prone to doubt.

Other questions gave more insight into the hearts of those who grew up in the church and yet do not regularly attend anymore. When we asked, "Is there any part of the church service that you miss today?" 72 percent of the holiday attendees said yes. (Only 27 percent of those who never attend said yes.) The Holy Spirit never gives up and will continue to challenge these 20 year olds due to this void in their spiritual lives. I believe the Holy Spirit is still speaking to these people. They feel the void. They know that something is missing. They know that the Church, for all its flaws, still has something to offer that they need.

Those who miss church gave a lot of different reasons. Some miss the teaching, some miss the special events. (Only about 7 percent said they missed the music, and nobody was missing Sunday school!) Most of them simply said, "I miss worshiping God." That's a powerful statement if you think about it — and it should remind us that we are dealing with souls and not statistics. In fact, it might be one of the most heart-breaking statements to come out of this entire survey: *"I miss worshiping God."* Of those who don't attend church anymore, half of them really do miss it. And of those who missed it, more missed "worshiping God" than anything else. Fifty Sundays of the year they choose to sleep in. But on Easter and Christmas, the pinnacles of Christian celebration, the lure is so strong that they can stand on the edge no longer, and they take their place in the corporate celebration of Jesus Christ.

Those Who Will Come Back When They Have Kids — and Those Who Won't

In our study, we wanted to probe another commonly held notion about those who leave the church. Most people believe that these young adults will be back when they have children of their own. According to the LifeWay survey,[1] 24 percent of those who return do so because "I had children and felt it was time for them to start attending." This reason was significantly more common for women than men (31 percent versus 13 percent). Also, 20 percent "got married and wanted to attend with my spouse." We wanted to find out much more, so we started with the following question:

"Do you expect to attend church regularly when you have children?"

Yes. 38%

Don't Know. 30%

No. 32%

---

1. http://www.lifeway.com/lwc/article_main_page/0,1703,A%253D165951%2526 M%253D201117,00.html.

These are fairly standard results. Other people who have re-searched this come up with about the same numbers. About four in nine expected to go back to their same denomination, perhaps even the church that they grew up in. So there was almost an even split there as well. Let's read a little bit more into that: it would appear that about half want to go back to their roots — back to the same commu-nity in which they grew up. This is where they are comfortable; this is the experience that they want to pass on to their children. The other half are clearly looking for a change. They want something different. If they go back to church, they're going to break ties with their old ways, burn some bridges with their old denomination, and chart out into some new territory.

Things got interesting when we compared these results to their lev-els of belief. Take a look at these results! Notice there is a significant correlation between believing in the creation account and whether they will come back! There is a tie between what they believe about Genesis and their attitude toward Christianity — which is understandable. If the authority of God's Word is undermined in the first book (Genesis, as we outlined in the previous chapter), this leads to a slippery slide of unbelief about the whole of the Bible.

Amazingly, the research also showed that of those who expect to come back to church, 77.7 percent believe that they are saved. Only 8.4 percent do not believe that they will go to heaven upon death! (The rest didn't know.) That's a huge number. The correlation between what they believe, how they view Scripture, and what they plan on doing is huge. If we can do a better job of teaching proper belief, we will at least increase the possibility that these kids will return after they have children. It seems pretty obvious to me that if we had done this in the first place, many of them might not have ever left!

So about a third said they were never coming back and about a third are planning on it. What about the rest? When asked whether or not they would return to church after they have children, 30 per-cent said that they "don't know." The "I don't knows" from most sur-veys tend to get overlooked. We tend to think that these people are

	Planning on returning	Never coming back
Do you believe all the books of the Bible are inspired by God?	76.4% said yes	41.9% said yes
Do you believe in creation as stated in the Bible?	92.1% said yes	47.8% said yes
Do you believe in the creation of Adam and Eve in the Garden of Eden?	91.3% said yes	50.6% said yes
Do you believe all the accounts/stories in the Bible are true/accurate?	58.5% said yes	16.8% said yes

apathetic ("I don't know" = "I don't care"). I see something else here. I see an opportunity. Consider this seriously. A third said yes, they're coming back, a third said definitely no — but in between is an equally large segment who is hanging in the balance. They sincerely haven't been able to make up their minds as to whether they're going to return or not.

Half of those surveyed have friends that still go to church. More than half have been asked by their friends if they want to go to church with them. That's very encouraging, and that's probably why they're thinking of coming back. And what an opportunity for those who go to church.

This is what I see: I see a window of opportunity that any church-goer can take advantage of. Two-thirds of the people who have left the Church are either *planning* on coming back or they might be *considering* coming back. All it might take is a sincere invitation from a friend to encourage them to make the jump. But this window of opportunity is slowly closing. Consider this result from one of the Barna surveys:

Even the traditional impulse of parenthood — when people's desire to supply spiritual guidance for their children pulls them back to church — is weakening. The new research pointed out that just one-third of twenty-somethings who are parents regularly take their children to church, compared with two-fifths of parents in their thirties and half of parents who are 40 years old or more.[2]

Two Questions, Two Groups

As you can see, we gained a lot of insightful information by asking the questions *Do you plan on returning to church after you have children?* and *Do you attend on Christmas or Easter?*

Because these questions are related, it's not surprising that respondents tended to answer them the same:

69 percent of those who plan on returning when they have kids also attend during the holidays

64 percent of those who do not plan on coming back never come on holidays

Based on these two questions, we can identify two groups that represent the extremes of those who have left the Church:

Group 1: Those who never come to church at all and who never plan on returning (20.7 percent of all surveyed)

Group 2: Those who come at Christmas and/or Easter and who plan on returning after they have children (26.4 percent of all surveyed)

---

2. Barna Research.

When we compare these two groups with their levels of belief discussed on the previous pages, very powerful correlations can be seen. Significantly, *belief in the Bible is a major predictor of behavior in both of these groups!*

Group 1 thinks that the service is boring, the agenda is too political, and that the Bible is not relevant. These people have a low level of belief in the Bible.

When reporting what they miss about church, those respondents in Group 1 said that they miss the music . . . but that's obviously not enough to persuade them to come back. They point to significant questions and scientific objections that they have with the Bible's reliability. They don't like the people and they don't believe the message, so there's really no reason for them to come back at all. *The Bible is irrelevant to them and the people are too.* They won't come back unless something changes on this level.

Group 2, on the other hand, has a much higher level of belief in the Bible. Three-quarters of them believe that they are saved and report relatively high levels of belief in biblical accuracy, authority, and history. The obvious point here is that *over half of the people who have left the Church are still solid believers in Jesus Christ.*

When asked what they miss about church, they report that they miss the pastor's teaching. What they object to, however, is hypocrisy, legalism, and self-righteousness. *The Bible is relevant to them, but the church is not.* This group needs to be convinced that Christians in the church are living by God's truth, and are living in a way that is relevant to their lives (such as being a positive influence on their children).

We could even create a separate subgroup from this group. Let's call it "Group 2+." This group represents a full 12 percent of all the people in the survey. *They answered every question about the Bible correctly and take a serious literal interpretation of the historical events in the Book of Genesis.* Many of them still come to church on Christmas and Easter, and many of them are planning on coming back after they have children. These are the ones who miss worshiping God the most. They were most turned off by the hypocrisy that they saw in the Church. It's likely that they have a growing disdain for this — or perhaps they have been personally hurt in some way because of it.

They see a great discrepancy between what the people are saying and the way that they are living; they may have been torn by what they heard a preacher preaching and what they saw him doing. I believe it very likely they have heard the pastor compromise in some way on Genesis — and they see this as hypocrisy when the Church claims to believe the Bible as the Word of God. These people want authenticity. They want grace, truth, and relevancy in the Body of Christ. They're not going to come back unless something changes on this level.

All of the people in this survey, to some extent, are having their hearts tugged on by the Holy Spirit. *Out of a thousand people, there was not a single person who gave us all the wrong answers all the time.* There were some items that everyone believed. They just couldn't suppress the truth that was in them. Even though they may not be walking in a spiritual Christian life, there might still be some light — a residual gleam — inside of them. They may have left the Church, but they still have a hope of the Church in them. If they find a church that is vibrant, authentic, defends the truth, stands solidly on biblical authority, and lives by the truth, they very well might come back.

There's one other interesting finding from this portion of the study that I want to bring up. In all honesty, I'm not exactly sure what to think about it, but the numbers are powerful enough — and the issue is so dominant in our culture — that it cannot be ignored. When asked this question, "Is premarital sex okay?" this is how many people answered yes:

Attend on holidays	Never attend
34.3	69.7
Plan on coming back	**Never coming back**
28.9	78.3

Wow. Those are huge numbers, but what do they mean?

- Is this group turned off by what the Bible has to say about premarital sex?

- Are they sexually active and feeling internal guilt and condemnation?

- Have they been shunned by the church because of their sexual activity?

- Have they been rejected by the church because of an unwanted pregnancy?

Without further study, we can only speculate. But this is certainly an area that deserves further research. The spread on these numbers is even greater than the spread regarding people's belief in the Book of Genesis (and yet, of course God's plan for male and female marriage is clearly founded in the Book of Genesis!). Clearly, something is going on here.

So we have Group 1 and Group 2, and their beliefs make all the difference. This key observation opens the door to powerful practical application. And that's what we're really trying to get to in the first place, isn't it? We know there's a problem out there; we now understand much better *who* is leaving the Church and *why* they're leaving the Church; but *what* do we do about it? Based on other questions that we asked in the survey, two general powerful application points can be made:

1. To defend and teach the Bible from the very first verse — the great need for practical and relevant apologetics teaching for all ages

2. To live an authentic, biblically based Christian life as individuals and as a church, so people will see Christ reflected in all that's done. Stop the hypocrisy!

In Part 2 we will expand on these two applications in great detail. *Be encouraged — there is much that can be done and there is much to do.* But before jumping in headfirst, we need to backtrack a little. In order to fully understand where it is that we need to go from here, we have to understand how we got here in the first place! Certainly, the decrease in the belief in the Bible and the embarrassing un-biblical atmosphere in many churches did not happen overnight. The spiraling descent can be described in one word: IRRELEVANCE. And by the time you finish the next chapter you will know exactly what that means and why it is so vital in the life of individuals and any church that wants to be relevant in the world and be a healthy, life-giving place to those who worship there.

Britt's Bit: Crunching Numbers

The fascinating and powerful thing about analyzing data and interpreting it correctly is that you can see things that are otherwise unseeable. If the research is done carefully and the numbers compared appropriately, the statistics allow us to describe behavior and also to understand the belief behind those behaviors.

One of the wonderful things about studying human behavior and the data collected from individuals is that you can sort and divide the data into subsets very quickly. The click of a mouse can instantly render visible data that was apparently invisible. Comparisons that took me days in 1979 can be accomplished almost instantaneously today. For example, in our survey we asked the question "Is there anything a teacher or professor did or said that caused you to doubt the contents of the Bible?" Depending upon their answers of either yes or no, we could separate the data to identify the true influences of those teachers or professors.

We interviewed 1,000 20 year olds and asked them 78 questions, which can give you an idea of how much information we could learn from these non-churched individuals. Their responses can be compared and contrasted *ad infinitum*. However, one should never become carried away with the amount of data they collect, but how it can be used to answer the questions facing Christian leaders like Ken Ham. Just because you can compare doesn't mean that there's always anything really important to discover. But if you are willing to dig around in the numbers, every once in a while you strike gold and discover some things that can change the course of your whole life (or, as in this case, two things that could change the course of the entire Church).

CHAPTER 4

The Short Road
to Irrelevance

> If I told you earthly things and you do not believe, how will
> you believe if I tell you heavenly things? (John 3:12).

Westminster Abbey will probably survive, at least for a while. While
other churches in England are being converted and bulldozed by the
dozens, this stunning and sprawling cathedral will continue to stand
tall. It was first built to house a group of Benedictine monks in A.D.
1065. For the last 900-plus years it has been attacked, renovated, des-
ecrated, and consecrated over and over, earning it a permanent place
in history. Century after century, architects and craftsman have been
adding to its grandeur. When I walk through the corridors beneath the
breathtaking expanses of Gothic and Romanesque architecture, I get
an entirely different feel than I did in the nearby church where only a
few gray-haired parishioners sat in the dusty front rows. Westminster
Abbey is alive with people and activity. Yes, it will survive — but not
necessarily for the right reasons.

Westminster is part monastery. Its religious life revolves around a daily pattern of worship, prayer, song, and the Eucharist. Until the 19th century, Westminster was the third seat of learning in England, surpassed only by Oxford and Cambridge. It was here that the first third of the King James Old Testament and the last half of the New Testament were translated. But the thousands of people who come to visit every day rarely stop to pray, worship, or contemplate the Scriptures, because the Abbey is also part museum. The architecture, artwork, and icons are timeless and priceless; the architecture is unsurpassed. The cathedral is also part mausoleum. The throngs of camera-clad, backpack-toting tourists that flock here come to see the graves of leaders in the fields of religion, literature, and science. It is a pilgrimage of sorts — people coming from around the globe to pay homage before the graves of the likes of Geoffrey Chaucer, David Livingstone, Charles Dickens, Sir Isaac Newton, and Charles Darwin.

Charles Darwin? The founder of modern evolutionary theory? Buried in the floor of Westminster Abby? It's hard to believe, but I have stood there and looked at the grave myself. Isn't this the man who popularized the philosophy of evolution taking place over millions of years? What is he doing in here? He not only abandoned his church, but he strategically introduced ideas that were contrary to God's Word. Isn't it strange that the man credited with founding modern evolutionary theory should be buried in the same place that the King James Version of the Bible was translated?

No, that's more than strange; it's symbolic — a powerful example of the short road that the Church has followed into irrelevance. A man who popularized a philosophy that hit at the very foundation of the Church (the Word of God) is honored by the Church and buried in the foundation of the Church. It is symbolic indeed.

Darwin's popularity in the UK earned him a place of prominence on their most popular currency, the ten-pound note.

The Short Road[1]

The root of the word "relevance" comes from the word "relate." In order for something to be relevant, it has to connect (or relate) to something that is real and important. The problem we are studying, of course, is that 60 percent of the students who grow up in the Church have lost that connection. As we said in the last chapter, they fall into two groups: Group 1 believes that the Bible is irrelevant; Group 2 believes that the Church is irrelevant (unless it's a holiday or it's time to take the kids).

---

1. Most of the ideas in this chapter are covered in much greater detail in my book *Why Won't They Listen?* (Green Forest, AR: Master Books, 2002).

What happened? How did we get here? I believe it all started when the Church gave us "millions of reasons" to doubt the Bible. The Book of Genesis gives us a clear account of the creation of the universe, of the world, and of everything that lives, including humanity. A simple, literal interpretation of these passages makes it clear that this creation took place in six days, with God resting on the seventh, just a few thousand years ago. This history, as it is written concerning the creation of the universe and life, including the first two humans, Adam and Eve, and their fall into sin with the consequence of death — is foundational to all biblical doctrines. This is the foundational history for the gospel.

In the late 18th century and in the early 19th century, however, the idea that the earth is millions and billions of years old (rather than about 10,000) began to emerge in the scientific community of Europe. It wasn't a new idea, actually. Throughout human history, numerous cultures from different points of the globe have considered the universe to be old or even eternal. Dr. Terry Mortenson's excellent book, *The Great Turning Point*,[2] chronicles what happened next. At that time, many church leaders in England led their churches to adopt the millions of years and add them into the Scriptures. Some did this by reinterpreting the days of creation as long periods of time; others adopted ideas such as the "gap theory," attempting to fit millions of years into a supposed gap between the first two verses of Genesis. The shift was not arbitrary; it was calculated — particularly by deists who were looking for a so-called scientific justification for rejecting the Flood of Noah's day as an explanation for the fossil-bearing sediments, and for rejecting biblical authority in total, as advocates of this millions-of-years age for the earth. They saw this as devastating to the Bible's account of creation and the Flood and its connection to fossil layers.

Darwin, based on his own writings, was never a believer, and of course readily accepted the millions-of-years ideas. This actually

---

2. Terry Mortenson, *The Great Turning Point* (Green Forest, AR: Master Books, 2004).

paved the way for Darwin to present his ideas on biological evolution. After all, one needs an incomprehensible amount of time to postulate the idea that small changes observed in animals will somehow add up to the needed big changes for Darwinian evolution — for reptiles to change into birds, for ape-like creatures to change into human beings, etc. Not only did the old-earth idea contradict what the Bible says, but because it is ultimately an attack on biblical authority, it paved the way for the conclusion that the Bible cannot be trusted, and our existence is the result of natural processes.

As the Church compromised on the issue of millions of years, subsequent generations were put on a slippery slide of unbelief. The millions-of-years idea not only undermined the creation account, but it began to undermine the historical account of the Genesis Flood as well. Soon the idea of a local flood rather than a global flood was popularized.

In 1859, Darwin published his major influential work, *On the Origin of Species*, and 12 years later *The Descent of Man*, popularizing the idea of the evolution of animals and the evolution of ape-like creatures into humans. Much of the Church in England (and then across the United Kingdom and Europe) began to also adopt Darwin's ideas, re-interpreting the Genesis account of creation and proposing views such as "theistic evolution" (that God used evolution to bring the different life forms into being).

Such views also spread to America, where various church leaders also adopted such positions to add millions of years and evolutionary ideas to the Bible's account of origins, thus reinterpreting the days of creation, the creation account of Adam and Eve, and so on. Even many conservative churches adopted the gap theory — seeing this as a way of rejecting evolution but allowing for millions of years.

Many conservative churches, which did not know how to handle the millions of years and evolutionary teaching, basically sidestepped the issues. They would (as they do today) teach Genesis as true, not dealing with the teachings of the secular world that contradicted the account (such as millions of years, evolution, etc.) — but teaching the account of creation, the Flood, the Tower of Babel, and so on as a wonderful story. They may claim it to be true — but, nonetheless, it is just taught to the students as a story.

The Church began to make a disconnection at this point. It was the beginning of the road to irrelevancy: the Church gave up the *earthly* things (e.g., the biological, anthropological, astronomical, geological history as recorded in Genesis 1–11) and focused on *heavenly* things (spiritual matters, relationships, the gospel). When it came to science, the Church gave in to human notions. It was now acceptable to use man's ideas to re-interpret the Bible, rather than to use the Bible to judge man's ideas. At times, the Church has tried to introduce hybrid theories that accommodate both secular science's interpretations and biblical accounts. The day-age theory and the gap theory are two examples. Unfortunately, they hold true to neither the scientific evidence nor the Bible!

The real consequence of such compromise can be seen in this quote from Ron Numbers, a modern scholar who stated the following in answer to a question for the media:

> For creationists, history is based on the Bible and the belief that God created the world 6,000–10,000 ago. . . . We humans were perfect because we were created in the image of God. And then there was the fall. Death appears and the whole account [in the Bible] becomes one of deterioration and degeneration. So we then have Jesus in the New Testament, who promises redemption. Evolution completely flips that. With evolution, you don't start out with anything perfect, you start with primitive little wiggly things, which evolve into apes and, finally, humans. There's no perfect state from which to fall. This makes the whole plan of salvation silly because there never was a fall. What you have then is a theory of progress from single-celled animals to humans and a very, very different take on history, and not just human history.[3]

---

3. Gwen Evan, "Reason or Faith? Darwin Expert Reflects," *Wisconsin Week*, Feb. 3, 2009, www.news.wisc.edu/16176.

In the past, the most highly recognized and progressive scientists in the field were also highly trained theologians (including Pascal, Newton, and Galileo). They helped maintain the connection between the Bible and science, between the laboratory and the sanctuary. We still have progressive scientists who are strong believers, but when someone comes to church today, they expect to hear about theology (the study of God). Do they expect to hear about biology, geology, and anthropology? The answer is no, of course. This is a major problem. Certainly the Church would not see itself as a research institution teaching people how to use microscopes or develop new electronics and so on. But this is where people have been confused. Observational science, which builds our technology, is very different to historical or origins science, which is concerned with the origin of what we observe in the present. It was the historical or origins science that the Church gave up to the world — and thus disconnected the Bible from the real world.

In America today, where do you go to learn about the geological, biological, anthropological, or astronomical history of the universe? School. That's where our kids learn what they perceive is the real stuff, the *relevant* stuff. In Sunday school they learn "Bible stories." (By the way, if you look at the definition of "story," it means "fairy tale." The Bible has become so irrelevant in our culture today that that's what most people think it is — just a spiritual "fairy tale.") What has taken its place? Charles Darwin's evolutionary ideas and the belief in millions of years for the age of the earth and universe are now, by and large, both *welcomed* and *honored* in the European church. And the Bible? It is seen as irrelevant when it comes to issues in the real world. The great disconnect between the Bible and "real" life has taken place. The Bible, God, and the Church became irrelevant in less than three generations. Generations have gone down this slippery slide of unbelief, until they have now basically rejected the entire Bible and its message of salvation.

What happened in Europe is happening on this side of the Atlantic today. We are on the same road — the same slippery slide — and we have traveled down it a long, long way. We may not be as far along as they are, but understand this: the exact same trend that took place in Europe is happening today. Our spirituality has become compartmentalized. Yes, we go to church, but only to get our emotional and spiritual needs met. Then we walk out the doors and face a pagan world where we have to live by a whole different set of assumptions. We might say this doesn't matter, but let's be honest: in the back of everyone's mind is the question *"If I can't trust the Bible in the earthly things, why should I trust it in the spiritual things?"* This was the same challenge Jesus Christ, our Creator and Savior, put to Nicodemus in John 3:12.

What really happened to the Church in the United Kingdom and Europe, and America — in fact, across the Western world — was that the Church basically disconnected the Bible from the real world.

Churches today in America are not a place where one talks about geology, dinosaurs, fossils, or the age of the earth — that is left up to the schools and colleges. Effectively, the Church basically hands over the history of the universe to the secular educational institutions, and concentrates on the spiritual and moral aspects of Christianity. The Church actually disconnects the Bible from the real world. The children (and everyone else, through Sunday school lessons, youth studies, etc.) in the churches are really taught that in church, one doesn't deal with geology, biology, and so on — that is for school. In church, we talk about Jesus — we deal with doctrines and we study moral and spiritual matters — but anything pertaining to understanding geology, biology, astronomy, anthropology, and so forth is left for school.

If I asked you where students go to learn about geology, astronomy, biology, and anthropology, what would you say? The answer is always "school." Please understand this! Ninety percent of children from church homes attend public/government schools.[4] There, by and large, they are taught a biological, anthropological, geological, and astronomical history of the universe that totally contradicts the Bible's account of creation, the Flood, and the Tower of Babel.

---

4. www.news.com.au/couriermail/story/0,23739,25375117-23272,00.html.

Yes, the epidemic has spread to our shores. Our current generation of children is leaving the church in droves. We are less than one generation away from being a nation of hollow, empty churches. It is more than possible that we will be the few, remnant gray-haired believers who sit in nearly vacant pews on Sunday.

President Obama summed it up in his autobiography, published just before his election as president of the United States of America:

> Whatever we once were, we are no longer just a Christian nation; we are also a Jewish nation, a Muslim nation, a Buddhist nation, a Hindu nation, and a nation of nonbelievers.[5]

Millions of Reasons to Doubt

A progression is taking place — a slow and steady decay of belief. I firmly believe that in this era of history the decay begins with the belief that the world is millions and billions of years old — because this is really where the major attack on biblical authority in this age began. Our survey reflects this trend in America.

- 77% believe in Noah's ark and the global Flood

- 75% believe in Adam and Eve in the Garden

- 62% believe that Abraham fathered Isaac when he was a hundred years old

- 60% believe in the Tower of Babel

- yet *only* 20% believe *that the earth is less than 10,000 years old*

The number-one area of disbelief is the age of the earth. Because of the five major issues we studied, four of the five have strong majorities, but very few believe the earth is truly less than 10,000 years old.

---

5. Barack Obama, *The Audacity of Hope: Thoughts on Reclaiming the American Dream* (New York: Crown Publishers, 2006).

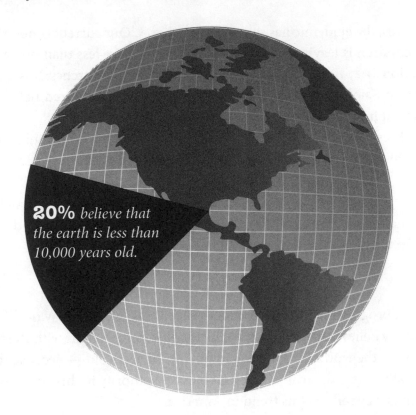

20% *believe that the earth is less than 10,000 years old.*

The age of the earth is the single most misunderstood issue among those who have left the Church. (It is also the most misunderstood issue among those who are still there!)

We live in an era where science has *supposedly* disproven the Bible in Genesis 1. What is the Church doing? Just like it did in Europe, it is sticking its head in the sand, compromising with the world.

Highly respected church leaders and theologians have given in. Many well-known Christian scholars, professors, evangelists, and the like have compromised the Bible with an old (millions-of-years) earth. You would probably be shocked if we placed a list of names here. Some of these Christian leaders have led many to Christ and have done a tremendous work in the spread of the gospel. Unquestionably, the ministry of these men has had a profound positive effect on multitudes of individual lives. Eternity has been changed because of their commitment and devotion to the gospel.

However, wittingly or unwittingly, they have been part of a vicious attack on biblical authority. Many would say that believing in millions of years is not important — as long as one accepts the gospel message about Jesus and His death and Resurrection. But as stated in chapter 2, the gospel message comes from the same book (the Bible) that records the Genesis account of history.

Recently a person was giving me an obvious dig at the ministry of AIG. He said, "The gospel doesn't rise or fall on the days of creation." My answer was, "That's true — it doesn't. But does the gospel rise or fall on the authority of Scripture? And does the authority of Scripture rise or fall on the days of creation?"

Faith in Christ alone saves — not whether a person believes in a young or old earth, or whether the days of creation are long periods of time. Romans 10:9 makes it very clear that salvation is tied to faith in Christ, *not the days of creation or the age of the earth*. There are many Christians (including many Christian leaders) who are truly saved, yet believe in millions of years and reinterpret the days of creation, or believe that God used evolution, or even that Noah's Flood was just a local event.

However, when a person believes in millions of years (or Darwinian evolution), and then reinterprets the days of creation to be long periods of time, they are undermining the very authority from which they get the message of the gospel. They are undermining the authority of the Word of God by taking man's fallible ideas on the age of the earth and using those ideas to change the clear meaning of the Word of God. It is an authority issue. Compromising Genesis has contributed to the loss of biblical authority in our nation and helped open the door to the secularization of the culture.

Here is a warning to any of us: if we teach such a compromised position to our children, be prepared for the great possibility they will open the door of compromise wider and get on that all-too-familiar slippery slide of unbelief. Believing in millions of years doesn't affect one's salvation, but it does affect how the next generation or those you influence view Scripture itself — and putting them on a slippery slide of unbelief has been the devastating consequence of such compromise.

It is interesting to note that many of these scholars who do compromise with millions of years agree that the obvious literal interpretation of Genesis shows that God created the earth in six approximately 24-hour days. Yet they adopt the interpretation of secular scientists regarding the age of the earth, rather than understanding that all dating methods are based on fallible assumptions and that it is God's Word that should be used to judge man's interpretation of the past — not the other way around. Whether we like to admit it or not, many of our contemporary champions of the faith are actually *undermining* the authority of the Bible (and thus the foundations of the Church) when they fail to defend what the Bible says about the age of the earth and the universe.

Our study showed that the majority of the people leaving the Church do not believe in evolution. This is actually the norm in our society as a whole. The universities and high schools are proclaiming evolution as an absolute fact. But after all their efforts, most people intuitively see it as false. Common sense tells them that something just doesn't "appear" by itself. Instinctively, human beings know that any complex organisms or mechanism must have an outside designer and creator to put them together. Those who take the time to study biochemistry, geology, physics, anthropology, paleontology, and genetics find even deeper problems within the idea of evolution. Many, many scientists have concluded that evolution couldn't have taken place, *no matter how much time was available.*

But the issue of the earth being millions of years old? This is the big stumbling block. When you go to zoos or museums, you see the issue of millions of years discussed (on signs, in videos, etc.) much more than you see the topic of evolution itself. History books, television programs, movie makers . . . everybody *assumes* that the earth and the universe are millions and billions of years old, so they *interpret* all the facts through that preconceived mindset. Then, when the Bible says that it happened in six days, they assume that the Bible is inaccurate, and that causes them to disbelieve the Bible more than any other single factor.

As I stated above, millions of years is really an incomprehensible amount of time — and you need an incomprehensible amount of time to even consider that evolution might have happened. When it comes to a major factor that has caused people to reject biblical authority, millions of years *is* the issue; it's not really evolution. If you can't believe in millions of years, you can't believe in evolution. In the 18th century, it was the age of the earth that caused the Church to begin to compromise the Word of God. This is why you have the day age theory, why you have the gap theory, why you have progressive creation. Each of these compromise positions on Genesis (as well as others) that are widely held in the Church, have one factor in common — supposedly fitting the millions of years in some way into the Bible's account of origins.

That's why Answers in Genesis is so passionate about defending the biblical account of creation in six days. People really can't believe, and don't want to believe, that their ancestors were apes. They look at the complexity of life forms and rhetorically ask, "How could we have come from a lifeless pile of slime . . . and where did the slime come from?!" But the issue of millions of years? That is so abstract and so incomprehensible that it's easier to accept. And since we've been told that it takes millions of years for something to evolve, then, in people's minds, it makes evolution plausible. Secular scientists need millions of years to make evolution happen. If they don't have millions of years, then the only alternative to explain our existence is to admit that there is an intelligent, personal force that created it in a relatively shorter period of time. Because most secular scientists believe in materialism (that only matter exists), they cannot accept the idea of "God." So, therefore, they must believe in millions of years — even though a proper interpretation of the evidence confirms that the earth is young, and that matter and life as we know it was created. Please visit our website if you haven't already! At www.answersingenesis.org you will find a tremendous amount of information and resources about this topic.

A belief that the earth is millions of years old, therefore, has two profoundly negative effects on people's beliefs:

1. It undermines the authority of the Book of Genesis and therefore the Bible as a whole.

2. It leaves open an excuse to justify that evolution could have occurred: given enough time, anything can happen.

Millions of years is the beginning of a slippery slope that slides down a predictable hill. When this happens, the authority of Scripture is compromised, and the authenticity of the Church is degraded. All across England — and now spreading from shore to shore in America — is an epidemic of unbelief with two major symptoms:

1. The Bible is no longer relevant to the skeptic because he/ she has not been taught convincing apologetics for its historical accuracy beginning at Genesis 1:1.

2. The believer has found the Church to be irrelevant because of hypocrisy, a watering down of God's Word, and an unwillingness to be flexible with cultural forms in order to stay true to the principles of God's inerrant Word.

A major shift has already taken place in our culture. If we don't recognize it, we will forever be wasting our time, energy, and resources as we try to maintain our churches and reach the world for Jesus Christ. The Church and the Bible are no longer the places we go to learn historical science. The Church gave up that responsibility and relegated it to the world. We kept the spiritual things, the moral things, and the relationships things. This is what most preachers will preach about, but is it relevant? Do young people today make a connection if it isn't connected to physical reality? I don't think so. We need to go back and rebuild the foundation of truth in God's Word. We need to be willing to shift our strategies in order to meet the needs in this new era. By understanding the times in which we live, we will have much clearer wisdom as we work toward a plan to be effective in this new world.

To the Jews and to the Greeks

On the first Easter morning, Jesus showed the world that He had victory over sin, Satan, and death. During the 40 days after the Resurrection, He appeared to the Apostles from time to time to affirm them, encourage them, and to prove that He really was alive. During one of those meetings, He told them that the Holy Spirit would come upon them and that they would receive power to tell people about Him "in Jerusalem, and in all Judea and Samaria, and to the ends of the earth" (Acts 1:8; NIV). Within hours of the Holy Spirit coming upon Peter and the Apostles, they were on the streets of Jerusalem witnessing to the Jews by explaining how the Old Testament prophecies about the Messiah had come true — and 3,000 of the Jews believed what Peter said. They were baptized and joined the Church (Acts 2).

After Paul was converted, he began to take the message of Christ beyond Jerusalem and the Jewish community. As he took the gospel toward the "ends of earth" and into the Greek world, it was a different story:

> A group of Epicurean and Stoic philosophers began to dispute with him. Some of them asked, "What is this babbler trying to say?" Others remarked, "He seems to be advocating foreign gods." They said this because Paul was preaching the good news about Jesus and the resurrection. . . . "You are bringing some strange ideas to our ears . . ." (Acts 17:18–20; NIV).

Life in Athens was different than it was in Jerusalem. Peter's approach for sharing the gospel with the Jews didn't work for Paul with the Greeks. So did Paul give up? Did he say, "There must be something wrong with these people. They are pagan unbelievers. They are resistant to the gospel. Their hearts are hardened and they are resistant to coming to church"? So he washed his hands and went back to Jerusalem. Right?

Wrong.

Paul must have realized that there was something wrong with his approach. We can see how he completely changed his strategy. He started out by actually complimenting these men for their religious fervor. He acknowledged their idols and then began to teach them about their own "unknown God" who was part of their culture. Where did he start teaching? He started at the beginning — first of all by defining God:

> The God who made the world and everything in it is the Lord of heaven and earth and does not live in temples built by hands. And he is not served by human hands, as if he needed anything, because he himself gives all men life and breath and everything else (Acts 17:24–25; NIV).

The Greeks believed in many gods. Paul had to back up and explain to them that there was only one true God. He had to show that this one true God created all things and gave life to all things. Then, building from that foundation, Paul could finally explain the gospel, telling them about repentance, about judgment, and about the resurrection of the dead. How did they respond? Some of them sneered; others wanted to hear more; and a few men became followers of Jesus Christ. Yes, life was different in Athens compared to life in Jerusalem. But Paul was willing to recognize this and change his entire approach to ministry because of it. When Paul wrote to the Corinthians about his experience, he noted this important distinction:

> But we preach Christ crucified: a stumbling block to Jews and foolishness to Gentiles (1 Cor. 1:23; NIV).

In Jerusalem, the Jews had a firm foundation belief built on the Old Testament. They knew about the one true God and about sin; they knew about the Law and about blood sacrifices for sin . . . and they already knew about the coming Messiah. Although many refused to believe, thousands accepted the message about Jesus on the spot and joined the Church. "Christ crucified" was a stumbling block that momentarily tripped them up, but many of them quickly got over it and made it to the other side. To the Greek, however, all this talk about Jesus and the Resurrection was considered utter foolishness. They had no previous knowledge about the one true God, about sin, or about the Law. Paul had to go back and start at the very beginning.

It's time to wake up and realize that a significant portion of the Western culture must now be considered "post-Christian." The godly foundation that once existed in England is now almost totally gone. That same foundation is faltering in America. Basic Christian concepts can no longer be taken for granted. Our culture *used* to be like Jerusalem. People used to have a basic understanding of biblical concepts and terminology. Someone like Billy Graham is well known for his basic presentation of the gospel. Some might take issue with his theology or methods, but there is no doubt that he could come into town, gather the masses in stadiums, and share about the death and Resurrection of Jesus Christ. Thousands would repent and receive Christ as their savior. Even Australia, my homeland, used to be this way. Students could recite the Lord's Prayer; they knew the Ten Commandments; they had respect for the Bible. When evangelists came through town, people were converted en masse.

In the Western world of today, the crusade approach just doesn't shake a city like it used to. Our culture today is much more like Athens. Yes, there is a remnant of understanding and respect for the Bible throughout this country, but in many ways, when you share the gospel with someone today you need to know that you're sharing with someone who is more like the "Greeks" and a lot less like the "Jews." The basic foundation of the Judeo-Christian heritage in this country *no longer exists*. It's *already gone*. If you take someone to a crusade or you give them a typical Christian tract, they are bound to say, "What is this babbler trying to say? . . . You are bringing some strange ideas to our ears."

Not so long ago, people used to say, "The Bible says it. I believe it. That settles it." That's not the case anymore. Today, the average guy on the street is more apt to say, "Who cares what the Bible says! I doubt it. That settles it!" Many Christians want to get the Ten Commandments back in school. But why should we expect the educators to post the Ten Commandments when they don't believe the book that it came from! Or if you give them a tract that says, "God loves you and has a plan for your life," they are likely to retort by asking, "Who is god anyway?" A generation or two ago there was at least a basic belief in the Christian God. Now you are likely to hear a slew of questions like this:

- How do you know God exists?

- Where did God come from?

- What about ape-men?

- How did Noah get all the animals on the ark?

- What about carbon dating?

The Bible is not taken seriously by those outside of the Christian Church today. Most courts have given up asking someone to place their hand on a Bible while taking an oath of truthfulness. Now we just swear by ourselves. Due to the lack of Christian training and strong Sunday school programs, many young people come out of high school untrained and unequipped to face the challenges presented by other teachers and professors. Due to their lack of training in apologetics and defending their personal faith, we now see these types of answers:

Nearly four out of five said they had instructors in school who taught them that the earth was obviously millions of years old.

Three out of five said their school instructors taught that life definitely evolved from lower forms of life to more complex forms.

About three in ten said they left high school believing that the Bible is less true.

Four out of five felt like their college professors had an ungodly influence on the students and imposed their philosophy and moral agenda.

One in three admitted that something that they were taught at an academic institution caused them to doubt the Bible. (We suspect this number is much higher — 20-somethings like to think that they make their choices independently, but this is almost never the case!)

When you consider all of the cultural influences that affect our thinking (including television, movies, museums, magazines, textbooks, and teachers and professors), it becomes pretty obvious that we are living in Athens and not Jerusalem.

When Billy Graham retired, I saw that as symbolic. It was the end of the era of the "Jews" and the beginning of the era of the "Greeks." We will not have another Billy Graham type of response in today's present culture. His message can't be heard the same way in this culture. *If they won't believe what the Bible teaches about earthly things, how will they believe about the heavenly things?*

I believe that this is one of the core problems behind the epidemic and the exodus of young adults from the Church. We've really been teaching only half of the truth — and the other half we gave up. We preach the gospel of the Crucifixion and the Resurrection. We preach about "trusting Jesus" and we preach about morality — but all the while, the attack on Genesis is raging, causing doubt, fueling unbelief, and *undermining every single thing that we say.*

In the wake, we are dealing with all sorts of peripheral issues, including homosexual behavior, abortion, relativism, school violence, and pornography. We are preaching about these things, but the truth is that the next generation doesn't believe when these things are preached against and biblical morality is taught, because they don't believe in the authority of Scripture. The Scriptures have become irrelevant to them; they don't make the connection between the spiritual, scriptural things and real, practical things.

The authority of the Scriptures is the foundation. If that is not protected, everything will eventually crumble. In honesty, isn't that where we already are? If we look at our schools, our churches, and our families we have to admit that the relevance of Scripture is already gone in this culture.

That's the bad news. When it comes to the Bible and the Church, we've taken the short road to irrelevance. The good news is that we can do something about it. Answers in Genesis exists to deflect these incoming attacks on God's Word so that when the life-changing messages of the Bible are proclaimed, they can be communicated with authority. When people believe what we say about the earthly things, they will be able to believe the things that we speak about the heavenly things. How do we do that? *By defending the Word, living by the Word, and standing on the Word uncompromisingly.* If we commit to doing these three things, relevance can be regained.

Britt's Bit: The College Fix?

Christian colleges are woven into the fabric of western Christianity. Parents often send their kids to a Bible-believing college for a lot of different reasons. Sometimes it is the desire of the students themselves — they want to grow in their faith and receive a faith-based education. More often than not, though, I find that it is the parents who want to send their children to a safe Christian environment. Many of these parents are desperately hoping that the experience and the teaching will increase their children's faith and make them align their lives along biblical principles. In some situations, parents insist that a Christian education is the only one that they will pay for. The kids don't want to go, but the parents say they have no choice.

Do Christian colleges help? If parents knew the truth, they would, in most instances, probably put their money somewhere else. In the last ten years, I have read 35 to 40 studies done for Christian educators. The results were so deplorable that they never allowed them to be published in the marketplace. In one such study, a Christian college wanted to compare itself with a nearby secular school to show that the moral atmosphere on their campus was superior to their secular neighbors. There was just one problem: after all the data was accumulated, they found only a very small, marginal difference in the morality of the students during and after college.

If we are going to stop the epidemic, it needs to happen in the Church and in the home during the elementary, middle school, and high school years. A Christian college experience can be a very positive thing for a growing Christian's faith. But the numbers indicate that parents must look at their children's early years in elementary and middle school to make sure they are prepared to defend their faith. Because if they don't, before they even get to college, they are already gone.

Part 2:
Solutions within Our Grasp

As the English philosopher Edmund Burke is purported to have said, "All that is necessary for the triumph of evil is for good men to do nothing."[1]

What a reminder from Simon Peter to "Always be prepared to give an answer to everyone who asks you to give the reason for the hope that you have."

Preach the word; be ready in season and out of season; reprove, rebuke, exhort, with great patience and instruction. For the time will come when they will not endure sound doctrine . . . they will turn away their ears from the truth and will turn aside to myths (2 Tim. 4:2–4).

---

1. thinkexist.com/quotation/all_that_is_necessary_for_the_triumph_of_evil_ is/205479.html.

CHAPTER 5

The Ready Defense

But in your hearts set apart Christ as Lord. Always be prepared to give an answer to everyone who asks you to give the reason for the hope that you have. Do this with gentleness and respect (1 Pet. 3:15; NIV).

Susan is in fifth grade and she loves it. Typical of children her age, her learning curve seems to be going straight up. She loves making friends; she loves reading books; she loves her mom and dad (though she's not sure about her big brothers that pick on her); and she loves Jesus . . . sort of. In all honesty, she's not too sure about Jesus right now. Yes, Susan grew up in the Church and faithfully attended with her family on a regular basis. For the last several years she has enjoyed the bliss of faith as a child. Now, however, on the verge of adolescence, she is beginning to make her faith her own . . . or not. Her spiritual life is hanging in the balance and no one even knows that's the case.

On Monday morning, with a ponytail sticking out from the side of her head and her favorite cartoon character embossed on her backpack, Susan will go to school.

At school, Susan learns many things. She learns about history, mathematics, language, and science — both observational and historical science. She learns the science from men and women who wear white coats and safety glasses. They use test tubes and Bunsen burners. They dissect animals and use microscopes to look at cells, and they carry clipboards under their arms to record all of their scientific findings. To Susan, they look smart. They do research. They test hypotheses. They prove them with their experiments. Susan knows that these people deal with real things — things that you can touch and feel — the kinds of things that matter. She spends many hours a week learning from these people. And she sees that *they are dealing with fact.* Because of this, when the same people talk about the history of the universe, dinosaurs, fossils, the origin of life, and the like, and interpret them in a particular way (e.g., millions of years and evolution) — Susan thinks they are speaking with the same authority as when they discuss their observational science that involves what you can observe and experiment with directly. Susan can't discern the difference between observational and historical (origins) science; to her, it is all science. And, that is how it is usually presented anyway.

On Sunday morning Susan's mom and dad will dress her up and take her to church. For two hours or so, she will enjoy the company of friends under the care of committed Christian volunteers. To Susan, they look nice. They read stories to her. She is not sure if they are true or not — but they are nice stories. They don't really connect to reality and they come from an old book anyway. They help her with her crafts. They sing songs together. Susan knows that these are good people and that they are teaching her about things that can't be seen. They tell her what to believe about many things. She actually has a 90 percent chance that her pastor and teachers will tell her that God created everything. (Only 10 percent of all the people in our survey, which again, attended conservative churches, said that their pastor said it was okay to believe in Darwinism.)

However, there is a very strong likelihood she will get the idea she can believe in millions of years. Yes, this is a Bible-believing church after all. Or they will tell her *what* the Bible says, but they don't tell her *why* to believe. No charts, no time-lines, no experiments. She's learning about things that she can't touch or feel, and she's not entirely sure anymore that these things really matter. All in all, Susan will get about ten minutes of focused, spiritual input from adults this week at church, and none of it will include science. And she knows that *they are dealing with faith.*

Over the next few years, Susan's "worldview" (her philosophy of life) will be formed. She doesn't even know this is happening, but connections and assumptions are being made in her mind that will determine how she interprets everything that goes on around her for the rest of her life. By ninth grade or so, she will be able to articulate her worldview to herself and others. She will even think she came up with her worldview herself, but that's not true. Her belief has mostly been shaped by all of the input that she has been getting throughout her childhood. What has she learned? She has learned about the facts that supposedly govern the world, and she has learned about the faith that supposedly governs the heavens. The problem is that many of the "facts" that she has learned seem to contradict her faith — but no one talks about those things at church.

In her mind, there are obvious questions that no one seems to be asking:

- Why is there death and suffering if God is a good God?

- Why can't people of the same sex who love each other get married?

- Isn't it better to get divorced than live unhappily?

- How can the earth be only a few thousand years old when it "looks" so old?

- Why is Jesus the "only way"?

- How come dinosaurs have nothing to do with the Bible or church?

Because no one asks these questions, she assumes that no one has the answers to these questions. She realizes that church people seem to have faith *in spite of* the "facts" that she has been told. That didn't matter so much as a child, but now on the edge of adulthood, she begins to feel the disconnect: *The facts are relevant; faith is not. If you want to learn something that's real, important, and meaningful, you do that at school. If you want to learn something that is lofty and emotional, you do that at church. At school, they teach about everything — fossils, dinosaurs, marriage (different views, gay marriage, etc.), sex, the origin of life, what is "right" and "wrong," different religions — they learn about everything!*

Yes, she's still in elementary school, but she is on her way to being one of the 20-somethings who will leave the church and never come back — not even during the holidays; not even when she has children of her own. She's not cynical, she's just skeptical. She's not uncommitted, she's just indifferent. She will become what George Barna calls "the Invisible Generation" that brashly challenges us to respond to her honest questions:

> All I want is reality. Show me God. Tell me what he is really like. Help me to understand why life is the way it is and how I can experience it more fully and with greater joy. I don't want empty promises. I want the real thing. And I'll go wherever I find that truth system. — Lisa Baker, age 20[1]

Susan is already sliding down the slope of unbelief. She's *willing* to believe in something that is real, but no one offers her anything like that on Sunday morning. They tell her *what* to believe, but they do not tell her *why*.

---

1. George Barna, *The Invisible Generation: Baby Busters* (Barna research group, 1992).

No one talks about it at home either. By and large, what she is taught at secular school is not dealt with. She is given no answers. Even at Christian school, the textbooks don't really teach answers to the skeptical questions of the day. And even in most homeschools, kids may be taught the Bible is true, but many don't understand how a non-Christian thinks, nor are they prepared to answer the questions of the day. In many instances, the same compromises with or indifference about millions of years and evolution are no different than the compromising churches. In the vacuum of answers, her doubts begin to solidify.

When did Susan's problems start? Did they start with television? Did they start with secular school? Did they start in Sunday school? Actually, her problems started a long, long time ago . . . a long time ago in a garden.

Defenseless

Adam and Eve had it made. In fact, I don't even think we can imagine the beauty, the harmony, and the intimacy that they shared with each other, with the world, and with God. It was all "very good," as God proclaimed. In unhindered exploration of God's creation, they walked freely in the Garden of Eden, "naked and unashamed," without fear, without condemnation, without threat. Yes, it was very good, but it didn't last. God placed only one parameter on Adam and Eve: "of the tree of the knowledge of good and evil you shall not eat, for in the day that you eat of it you shall surely die." (Gen. 2:17).

The serpent in the garden was more sly than anything else that God had made. Having rebelled against God and having been thrown down from heaven, Satan laid down the doubt that would lead to the sin that would distort, decay, and bring death to the perfection that God had created. It was a simple and subtle scheme. It wasn't a direct accusation at first — just a hint of a suggestion. It was the beginning of doubt — the same doubt that plagues the generation that is now exiting the Church. Satan simply brought up a slight possibility:

Did God *really* say, "You must not eat from any tree in the garden? . . . You will not surely die" (Gen. 3:1–4; NIV, emphasis added).

Did God really say . . . ? It was the first attack on the Word of God. Since then, the attack has always been on the Word of God. The attack manifests itself in different ways during different areas of history. But the question is really always the same. *Did God really say . . . ?* Throughout the centuries, Satan has attacked the Word of God and attacked the human soul by casting doubt into the truthfulness of what God has said and the relevance of God's words in practical everyday life. In the last 100 years, the attacks have begun to sound more and more scientific:

- Did God really say that He created everything? Surely science has proven that the big bang happened spontaneously, without any outside force.

- Did God really say that He created the earth in six days? Surely science has proven that life evolved over millions and billions of years.

- Did God really say that He created life? Surely science has proven that the right chemicals in the right place over a long enough period of time will spontaneously generate living forms.

- Did God really say that He created humanity? Surely science has proven that the human race is really just a highly evolved life form that is the product of time and random chance.

- Did God really send a worldwide Flood in the time of Noah? Surely science has shown there never was a global Flood, and that the fossil layers were laid down over millions of years — not by a Flood.

The youth of today are wrestling with such questions. Fact seems to disprove faith. As we saw in the last chapter, how did the Church respond to this attack in England? By doing almost nothing. Actually, they did do something — they basically agreed one could accept the teachings of the world concerning the past, and reinterpret the Bible's account in Genesis. It focused on issues of faith and left its people defenseless against the so-called facts. To a certain extent, evangelical Christianity has done the same thing in America. Oh, yes, there are a few people in every congregation who seem to specialize in "apologetics." They are the brainiacs who read and study and seem to have a quick answer for everything. But they are few and far between. The rest of us try to ignore our doubts, leave the intellectual battles to someone else, and just focus on Jesus and the gospel.

But in this day and age, we must see that an attack on the Word of God *is* an attack on the gospel. Without the Word of God, we have no gospel. Without the Word of God, we have no morality. Without the Word of God, we have no record of our past and no prophecy for our future. Without the Word of God, Christianity cannot stand.

Biblical Authority Issues

Those of us who are born-again Christians believe that Jesus Christ bodily rose from the dead. After all, as Paul states in 1 Corinthians 15:14: "And if Christ has not been raised, then our preaching is vain, your faith also is vain." We believe, as real historical fact, that Jesus Christ bodily rose from the dead.

But let me ask you a question: how do you *know* Jesus Christ rose from the dead? You were not there, and you don't have a movie re-run, so how do you know? Because the Bible says, that's how. We accept that the Bible is the revealed Word of God — it is inerrant, inspired, the "God-breathed" revelation from our Creator. And as such, we let God's word speak to us through this written Word. If it is history, we take it as history. We don't try to force our ideas onto God's Word; we let it speak to us in the language and context in which it is written. How about Jesus actually walking on water? Or that Jesus fed thousands of people from just a few loaves and fishes? Or that Jonah was swallowed by a great fish? We know, because it's in the Bible.

But if I go to many churches in America and ask if God created everything in six ordinary days, that death of animals and man came after sin, that there was a worldwide Flood in the time of Noah and so on, I suddenly get responses like, "Well, we wouldn't say that. The days could be millions of years. God could have used evolution. Noah's Flood might have been a local event or really didn't make much impact on the earth," and all sorts of similar statements.

Now I want you to understand what has happened — this is key to understanding what has happened to our culture, and key to understanding why our kids are leaving the Church. This is the crux of the issue. It is an issue of authority — biblical authority.

It is true that the literal events of Genesis are foundational to all doctrine — to the gospel. In Matthew 19:4–7, when Jesus was explaining the doctrine of marriage, He quoted from the creation account of Adam and Eve to teach the doctrine of one man for one woman. The whole meaning of the gospel is dependent upon the account of the Fall of man, and thus original sin, as given in Genesis. Ultimately, every single biblical doctrine of theology, directly or indirectly, is founded in the historical account given in Genesis 1–11. And Genesis is written as typical historical narrative (not like the Psalms that are written as typical Hebrew poetry). If one undermines this history, or reinterprets it, or tries to claim it is myth or symbolic, then one undermines the foundation of the rest of the Bible, including the gospel.

But even given this, there is something far more crucial — it is the very WORD itself, the authority of the book we call the Bible.

The reason we know Jesus rose from the dead is that we take God's Word as written. The reason we know a fish swallowed a man is that we take God's Word as written. And if you take God's Word as written in Genesis (and it is written as history and quoted from as history throughout the Bible as did Jesus Himself in His earthly ministry), it is very clear that God created in six ordinary days, that man and animals were vegetarian before sin, there was a global Flood, and there was an event after the Flood called the Tower of Babel that formed the different people groups.

Thus, one can't have a fossil record of supposed millions of years before man containing evidence of animals eating each other, bones with diseases like cancer, and thorns said to be hundreds of millions of years old, when everything was described by God as "very good" and animals and man were vegetarian and there was no sin and thus no death and disease or thorns before Adam's rebellion. The ultimate reason so many in the Church (including professors at Bible colleges, seminaries, and Christian colleges) reinterpret the Genesis account of creation, or say it is not important, is because of the influence of the idea of millions of years and evolutionary teaching.

Here is the point. Stand back and consider the big picture. If we teach our children (or anyone) to take God's Word as written concerning the Resurrection, the miracles of Jesus, and the account of Jonah and the great fish that swallowed him but then tell them we don't need to take Genesis as written but can reinterpret it on the basis of the world's teaching about millions of years and evolution — we have unlocked a door.

The door we've unlocked is the door to undermine biblical authority. We are really saying, "We want you to take God's Word as written according to literature and language in certain places — but not here at the beginning in Genesis." What we have actually done is made man the authority over God's Word. We have taught our children that they can take what they learn at school and can reinterpret the Bible's clear teaching in Genesis to supposedly fit this into the Bible. By staying silent and not defending Genesis, we are "teaching" our children that we don't have to take God's Word as written, and man can reinterpret God's Word according to what the majority in the culture might believe.

Scripture teaches that if there is sin or compromise in one generation and it is not dealt with, it is usually observed to occur to a much greater extent in the next generation, and so on. When we unlock that door in Genesis, the next generation usually pushes that door open farther — and then the next generation farther again, and then the next farther again — until eventually all of the Bible is rejected. There is a loss of biblical authority each generation until it becomes an epidemic throughout the Church and nation. The structure of Christianity (its morality, its Christian worldview) collapses, to be replaced by a man-centered structure where moral relativism would pervade the culture. That is what we have seen across Europe, and before our very eyes in America.

An Open Door

So why do we tolerate ideas that undermine the authority of God's Word? We think that simply because a secular humanist or an atheist is not directly attacking Jesus or the Cross that he's not attacking them at all. If the mass media and education systems directly targeted Jesus and the Resurrection, most in the Church would be up in arms. But if the foundation of those beliefs is attacked and weakened first (the attack on the Word itself), then unbelief creeps across the country and through the Church slowly and surely, while we have to fight more and more for the things we value in our faith.

Many Christian organizations are spending millions of dollars and countless hours trying to change the culture. We are trying to get nativity scenes back on public grounds. We are trying to get the Ten Commandments back in the courtrooms. We're trying to get the Bible back in the classroom. (Actually, I don't think that's true. I don't think anyone even *hopes* that the Bible might someday be read and respected in the secular schools anymore.) But why in the world would the Bible (and its Ten Commandments, nativity scenes, and so on) be allowed in the classroom if the educators don't believe it's true. And the gospel? The message of Jesus comes from the same book that records the Genesis history of creation and the Flood. If they don't believe in the first part (which is written as history and quoted as history throughout the Bible), why would they believe in the rest?

The world, the devil, and even our sinful human tendencies have caused a deep, dark shadow of doubt to fall across God's Word. *Did God really say . . . ?* In regard to the events in Genesis — six literal days, and so on — most people would say no, because the Word of God has been under successful attack. In Europe the attack began when scientists threw doubt on the age of the earth. In America today, those same attacks are shattering the foundation upon which the Church and the gospel depend. Actually, the Bible itself warns us that such attacks will happen and we need to be ready for them. In 2 Corinthians 11:3, Paul warns us that Satan will use the same attack on us that he did on Eve:

> But I am afraid that, as the serpent deceived Eve by his craftiness, your minds will be led astray from the simplicity and purity of devotion to Christ.

And what was the method used on Eve? *"Did God really say . . . ?"* He got Adam and Eve to doubt and thus disbelieve the Word of God. This attack was meant to cause Adam and Eve to reinterpret God's Word based on their own appraisal of things. They looked at the evidence — the beautiful fruit — and decided that God's Word couldn't mean what they thought it meant. It was okay to reinterpret it and determine truth for themselves. I call this "the Genesis 3 Attack"! Genesis 3 Attacks have occurred over and over again throughout history. And in this era (particularly since the late 18th century), the Genesis 3 Attack has manifested itself as science attempting to disprove the account of creation, the Flood, and the Tower of Babel in Genesis. Our culture today is in great danger — the Genesis 3 Attack has hit the Church and the culture!

While I have very strong feelings about the direction that our culture is going, I do not believe that culture can be changed from the top down. Sure, you might get the laws changed for the next four years, but the next guy who gets voted in can erase everything. You might be able to win a few legal battles regarding freedom of speech, but before we know it, the next group will be telling us to sit down and shut up.

Why? Because they don't believe the book from which we speak. You see, the culture has changed from the foundation up, as reflected in the predominant secular worldview and relative morality. The culture went from being built on the foundation of God's Word to being built on the foundation of man's word. And this has also happened in the Church. When the Church adopted millions of years and evolutionary ideas into the Bible, they put man in authority over God's Word, making man the ultimate authority, not God! No wonder the kids are walking away from the Church!

At its heart, Answers in Genesis is not a creation-versus-evolution ministry, and we're not out to change the culture. The Bible doesn't say to go into all the world and change the culture, but to go into all the world and preach the gospel. The culture changed because hearts and minds changed in regard to the Word of God. To change the culture back, hearts and minds need to be changed toward God and His Word. When such changed hearts and minds, committed to the Word of God, shine light and distribute "salt" in the culture — then the culture will change.

We see it as our job to defend the Christian faith, stand on the authority of God's Word without compromise, and proclaim the gospel of Jesus Christ. And when the relevancy of the Word of God is restored, lives will be changed as the power and authority of the living Word of God empowers their lives. Then, we believe, these individuals will permeate the culture by living truthfully and honestly in harmony with godly principles . . . and *then* culture will be changed from the bottom up. That's what this ministry is all about. We strive to get information out there to change the foundation and worldview of individuals so the culture will naturally be changed from the heart.

We forget that the first attack by Satan was to cast doubt on the Word of God. How does that relate to the gospel today? Paul shared his concerns in the verse quoted previously from 2 Corinthians 11:3:

> But I am afraid that, as the serpent deceived Eve by his craftiness, your minds will be led astray from the simplicity and purity of devotion to Christ.

Satan deceived by his craftiness, the Word of God was compromised, and people's minds were corrupted from the simplicity of the gospel and Jesus.

But why should we be surprised? Psalm 11:3 says, "If the foundations are destroyed, what can the righteous do?" Our foundation is the Word of God. We need to defend the Word of God as one of our top priorities as Christians. If we are to give a strategic and effective response to the wave of souls who are leaving the Church, these issues must be addressed.

The Attack Today

In our survey, we asked the thousand young adults who have left the Church if they believed that all the accounts and stories in the Bible are true and accurate. Of those, 44 percent said no, 38 percent said yes, and 18 percent didn't know. We asked those who said no this follow-up question: If you don't believe all the accounts and stories in the Bible are true and accurate, what made you begin to doubt the Bible?

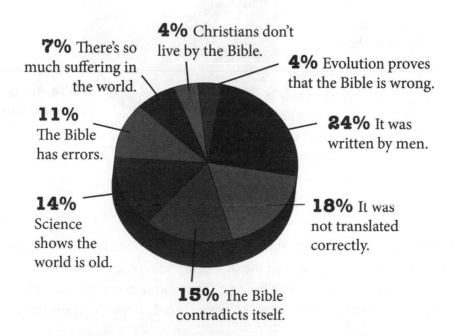

7% There's so much suffering in the world.

4% Christians don't live by the Bible.

4% Evolution proves that the Bible is wrong.

11% The Bible has errors.

24% It was written by men.

14% Science shows the world is old.

18% It was not translated correctly.

15% The Bible contradicts itself.

Look at those results again. If you add up all of the responses related to biblical authority, you'll see that 82 percent of those who said they did not believe all the accounts and stories in the Bible are true and accurate did so because of doubts about the authority of the Bible. Then we asked this other question: Does the Bible contain errors?

Forty percent said yes and another 30 percent didn't know. Only 30 percent said that the Bible does not contain errors. Of those who said that the Bible does contain errors, these were the supposed errors that they pointed out:

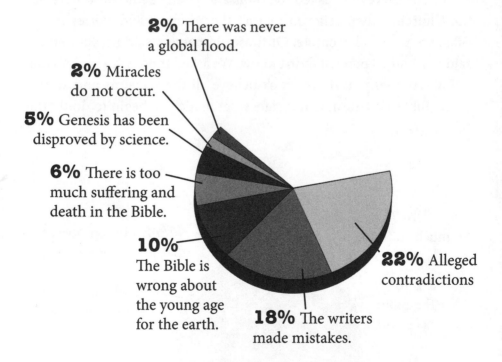

2% There was never a global flood.

2% Miracles do not occur.

5% Genesis has been disproved by science.

6% There is too much suffering and death in the Bible.

10% The Bible is wrong about the young age for the earth.

18% The writers made mistakes.

22% Alleged contradictions

These are the doubts that students like Susan are facing. These are the doubts that are plaguing the hearts of the next generation. For the group that will never come back to church and never comes on holidays, these issues are even more pronounced. It would seem logical, then, that if we are to strategically respond to the devastating epidemic of young adults who are leaving the evangelical Church, we should be addressing these issues. Responding to these attacks on our Bible should be at the forefront of our attempts to restore relevancy to the Word of God and make our churches relevant to this generation. It is so obvious we need to be teaching apologetics in our churches — creation apologetics and general Bible apologetics! The fact that this is not happening in the majority of our churches, nor in the majority of Bible and Christian colleges and seminaries, is one of the great travesties of this age in regard to the Church.

What is really happening?

A False Relevancy

Medical researchers often talk about a phenomenon called "the placebo effect." When trying to determine the effectiveness of a drug or treatment, sometimes researchers will intentionally give a group of people a pill that looks like the new medicine but really isn't. Amazingly, the people taking the false medicine sometimes *feel* better even though the pill is not actually helping them at all.

A similar thing is happening in the Church. In our efforts to slow the flood of young adults who are leaving, we often give the Church a placebo. We try to restore *cultural* relevancy without restoring *biblical* relevancy. As you'll see in the next chapter, I'm all about adopting religious forms that are appropriate to the culture of the upcoming generation. Becoming "culturally cool" can feel like it helps for a while, but it's really just a placebo, a Band-Aid for a much deeper disease. By simply making our services more attractive to the younger generation, we might feel better and they might feel better, but it's doing nothing to solve the core issue of the epidemic. All it does is sacrifice eternal truth for short-term attractiveness, and it turns a church into an organization that is driven by the felt needs of its young consumers.

Tell them what they want. Make them feel good. That's not what the doctor ordered. Yes, we need a good bedside manner, but the Church is sick and it needs to be told the truth — and they need to know that the truth hurts sometimes. (Okay, *a lot* of the time.)

One of my big frustrations with this "placebo effect" comes down to music. I have visited hundreds and hundreds of churches. Everywhere I go, music seems to be the central issue. Even in conservative churches everyone tries to make a big deal out of praise and worship. We think that if we can make it dynamic, energetic, and fit the style of the generation we're trying to reach, the epidemic will be stopped and young people will start flooding back into the Church. That's simply not the case. Our research showed that music is *not* a fundamental factor in young adults choosing to leave or stay at a church — but the preaching of God's Word is.

Now don't get me wrong. David used music to praise the Lord. God has created us to love music. We can use music to worship the Lord. But what I'm talking about is the fact that music is seen by many in the church as the most important part of the service — that it is the music that will draw people in. This is not what our research showed. Yes, people love music, but they want good teaching!

However, to try to restore relevancy to Scripture, what do we usually do these days? We add guitars and drums to the service. We think that the Church needs to follow the culture in order to be relevant. But cultural forms do not make you relevant, they just make you cool. Truth makes you relevant. It doesn't mean we can't make such reforms to be more contemporary — but the motive and priority are what is so important.

I watched an argument one time between the worship pastor and an associate pastor over how much time I would have to speak in the service. I was trying to get my computer set up, but I guess I was interfering with the rehearsal. The worship pastor got a little bent out of shape and told the other pastor, "Hey! Music is the most important part of this service!" Eventually the other pastor backed down. That day we had 20 minutes of praise and worship, 20 minutes of message, and 25 minutes of worship at the end. The Word of God was put in second place. The placebo was given precedent; the real medicine was given a token amount of time. I see that everywhere, by the way — in liberal churches, conservative churches, across all denominations. And besides, many times the music worship time is more of a stage production and entertainment time than it really is a worship time.

There is a war going on over the Word of God. This is not the time to focus on making people feel good. Through our survey, we can now better pinpoint the areas where they are struggling with doubt.

Resources for Reclaiming Biblical Relevance

Let's take another look at the situation that the first-century Apostles were facing and draw another parallel between their situation and ours today. Is a child like Susan growing up in Athens or is she growing up in Jerusalem? In other words, is she growing up as a "Jew" in a society where biblical belief is assumed, or is she growing up in a "Greek" society that is secular and skeptical?

The answer is that Susan is actually doing a little of *both*. Part of her is growing up in a church that believes. Christianity is the accepted norm on Sunday morning. The problem is that the moment she steps out the door, she enters a world that is more like Athens. Because of that, Susan's church should be "equipping the saints for the work of the ministry" in an unbelieving world by teaching her and her church to defend the Word of God from the very first verse against the skeptical attacks of this age. Not only would this help protect Susan's faith from the attacks she gets in the world, but it would also arm her and the rest of her congregation to take the offensive. In both situations, the foundation of the authority of the Word of God both inside and outside the Church needs to be rebuilt.

The Church needs to be reminded over and over why the majority of students begin to doubt the Bible in middle and high school — and then *diligently* deal with the issues by introducing relevant apologetics courses (teaching a logical, reasoned defense of the faith) by at least middle school (even before).

As I travel around the world teaching on biblical apologetics, I find that whether my audience is primarily secular or Christian, regardless of what country I'm in, I get asked the same basic questions — such as (to name only some of them):

- How do you know the Bible is true?

- Hasn't science disproved the Bible?

- Isn't the world millions of years old?

- What about carbon dating?

- How did Noah get all the animals on the ark?

- But don't we observe evolution because we see animals change — we see bacteria become resistant to antibiotics?

- If God created Adam and Eve, only two people to start with, where did all the people come from?

- How come there are so many different "races" of people?

- But dinosaurs don't fit with the Bible; how do you explain them?

- Where is the evidence for a global Flood?

- How can you believe in a loving God when there is so much death and suffering around us?

Most Sunday school lessons, sermons, Bible studies, etc., are not teaching people how to answer the questions of the day. They are not connecting the Bible to the real world. They are not teaching people how to defend their faith — and we wonder why we are losing them. Not only is apologetics (a logical defense of the faith) not taught in most churches and Sunday schools, it is not taught at most Bible colleges or seminaries — or is actually taught against! Church leaders today seem to think that programs, entertainment, music, and many other things are what is needed to reach people and keep them in church.

However, our research also showed something very different — that people want good Bible teaching. It is the preaching of the Word and making it relevant to them in today's world that they need and want. But this is not happening even in Sunday school in the majority of instances, let alone the rest of the church programs.

The Bible is not some "pie in the sky" philosophical book. It's a real book that is really connected to the real world. It is a history book that connects to dirt, fossils, stones, bones, tsunamis, earthquakes, oceans, mountains, death, and so on. It has *everything* to do with geography, biology, anthropology, and sociology. The Word of God has never changed, but the Church's perception of the Word of God changed when it failed to engage the scientific community on matters of fact as well as faith. It's time to change that and be true to the challenge that Peter left for each of us to follow:

> But in your hearts set apart Christ as Lord. Always be prepared to give an answer to everyone who asks you to give the reason for the hope that you have. Do this with gentleness and respect (1 Pet. 3:15; NIV).

Typical churches use materials that are more geared for "the Jew in Jerusalem" who has a developed religious background and lives in a religiously friendly society. That's just not the case anymore. Our society is now immersed in secularism. It's absolutely essential that we learn to defend the Bible and the Christian faith for the sake of our faith and our children's faith, and to evangelize a society that has a highly diminished understanding of biblical truth. I firmly believe that we are now in the era of the "Greeks" . . . yet our churches and Sunday schools are still teaching us like "Jews." See the problem?

We do not have a ready defense in most of our churches — *yet*. But, thankfully, God has supplied us with all the weapons and shields we need to defend ourselves and to take the offensive in reclaiming the relevance of God's Word in our churches and in this society. Our defense must be strategic. As families and as a Church, we need to think through the threats that lurk around us and be willing to protect our families and our churches from the onslaught of ideas that continually cause us to question if God really said what He says He did.

I'm advocating a completely new approach to how we educate ourselves as Christians! God's Word and the Christian faith *are* supported/confirmed by the facts. The disconnect between faith and fact is nothing but an illusion created by an overwhelming misinterpretation of the facts. Good observational science *supports* faith. It always has and it always will. It's time to bring the facts back into our faith. Training yourself, your family, and your church to be defenders of the faith is an exciting and empowering adventure. It can change the Church — it can change the world. It's time to attack doubt with courses and preaching and teaching that defend God's Word against the attacks of this age!

That sounds like a huge endeavor, and in some ways it is — in fact, it will take a *lifetime!*

But thanks to this survey, we now know where we need to focus our efforts *today*. We now know which lies are causing elementary, middle school, and high school kids to doubt the most:

- The Bible was written by men.

- The writers made mistakes.

- It was not translated correctly.

- The Bible contradicts itself.

- The Bible has errors.

- Evolution proves that the Bible is wrong.

- The Bible is wrong about the young age for the earth.

- Genesis has been disproved by science.

- There is too much suffering and death in the Bible.

When we interpreted all the data, questions arising about the Book of Genesis represented about 40 percent of all the concerns. Ultimately, if we are unable to defend Genesis, we have allowed the enemy to attack our Christian faith and undermine the very first book of the Bible. We need to be able to defend our faith from general attacks *and* defend against the specific attacks on the Book of Genesis. The number of resources now available is wonderful. To get you started, however, let me give you a manageable, balanced arsenal of shields and swords that you can use to arm yourself and your family and your church.

God's Word stands by itself and doesn't need defending — that is true — but, practically, in this culture we are talking about answering the skeptical questions to *uphold* the Word and proclaim why we can believe in the Bible's life-giving historical and scientific authority. That means we need to not only know the Bible, but we need to know *about* the Bible and why it is worthy of our complete faith. Do you see why that's so important now? Some great resources to get you started are listed in appendix 3.

This Sunday, take a second look at the kids coming through the door of your church. Like Susan, most will appear to be excited, enthusiastic, and engaged. The fact is, about 30 percent of them are kids who are beginning to wrestle with significant doubts about the relevancy of the Word of God. What can we do to help children like her? What can we do to protect our own kids as well as our own hearts from the attacks on God's Word? By defending and teaching the Bible from the very first verse and then depending on God to keep us faithful to our call!

CHAPTER 6

The Real Deal

And He said to them, "Rightly did Isaiah prophesy of you hypocrites, as it is written: 'THIS PEOPLE HONORS ME WITH THEIR LIPS, BUT THEIR HEART IS FAR AWAY FROM ME. BUT IN VAIN DO THEY WORSHIP ME, TEACHING AS DOCTRINES THE PRECEPTS OF MEN.' Neglecting the commandment of God, you hold to the tradition of men" (Mark 7:6–8).

In the last chapter, we addressed the absolutely essential need to defend the Christian faith/Word of God in order to restore relevancy to Group 1, the young adults who have left the church, never come on holidays, and never plan on returning. But that leaves the other half, Group 2: those who come at Christmas and/or Easter and who plan on returning after they have children. Compared to Group 1, this group has a much higher level of belief in the Bible. Three-quarters of them believe that they are saved, and the vast majority of them report relatively high levels of belief in biblical accuracy, authority, and history. The obvious point here is that *over half of the people who have left the Church are still solid believers in Jesus Christ*. What they object to, however, is hypocrisy, legalism, and self-righteousness. *The Bible is relevant to them, but the Church is not.*

Researcher George Barna highlights this problem:

> Loyalty to congregations is one of the casualties of young adulthood: twentysomethings were nearly 70% more likely than older adults to strongly assert that if they "cannot find a local church that will help them become more like Christ, then they will find people and groups that will, and connect with them instead of a local church." They are also significantly less likely to believe that "a person's faith in God is meant to be developed by involvement in a local church."[1]

We have to be honest: at least half of those who are leaving the Church haven't left the faith; they have left the fellowship. They wouldn't see it as a Bible problem (even though they obviously have issues that need addressing), but a church problem. As a result of all this number-crunching and data analysis, we strongly advocate that Christians and the Church everywhere begin to *defend the Word*. Yet defending the Bible is *not* our end goal. It's really just the beginning. When someone is convinced of the relevance of God's Word, they must then make a commitment to *live the Word*. Our concerns are twofold:

1. The "Church" has become an institution that no longer reflects the characteristics and priorities described in the Word of God.

---

1. "Most Twentysomethings Put Christianity on the Shelf Following Spiritually Active Teen Years," Barna Group, September 11, 2006, http://www.barna.org/barna-update/article/16-teensnext-gen/147-most-twentysomethings-put-christianity-on-the-shelf-following-spiritually-active-teen-years.

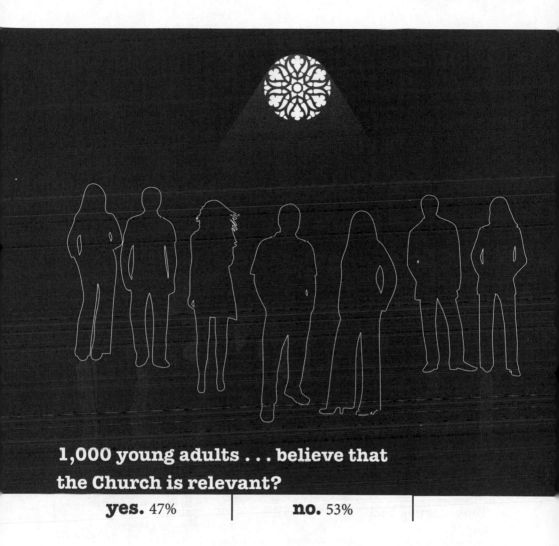

1,000 young adults . . . believe that the Church is relevant?

yes. 47% | **no.** 53%

When we asked the entire 1,000 young adults whether or not they believe that the Church is relevant, only 47 percent said yes, and a full 53 percent said no/don't know. And quite frankly, it's not just the 20-somethings who feel this way. In the book *Why Men Hate Going to Church*,[2] David Murrow addresses another major concern in church demographics: the Church is losing men as well as it is young adults.

2. David Murrow, *Why Men Hate Going to Church* (Nashville, TN: Nelson Books, 2005).

Men think church is irrelevant, too. The questions that young adults and men ask on Sunday mornings are *So what? Why should I go? If church doesn't work for me, what difference does it make?*

    2. People within the Church are not living authentically Christian lives based on the Word of God.

About two-thirds of the people in Group 2 actually think that the Church *is* relevant. But they still don't go. Why is that? It seems to be more a matter of *heart* issues than *head* issues. Relationships with people (rather than relationships with God) seem to be the stumbling block.

"Do you feel the Church is relevant to your needs today?"

	Yes	No & Don't Know
All surveyed	47%	53%
Easter and/or Christmas attenders	60%	40%
Those coming back with kids	74%	26%

Notice that those who feel the Church is most relevant to their needs are those who intend to come back when they have kids. Not only do they see the value of the church experience for their children, but it's quite possible that they also know that the people they're having difficulty with will have moved on by then! Just to verify the results of that question, we asked this question:

"Do you feel good people don't need to go to church?"

	Yes	No & Don't Know
Easter and/or Christmas attenders	33%	67%
Those coming back with kids	27%	73%

Isn't this interesting! At least two-thirds of those who go to church on holidays and plan on coming back feel like good people *do* need to go to church . . . and yet they don't go regularly themselves! Why is that? I believe it's because the Church, and oftentimes the individuals in it, are not living by the Word in at least three critical areas: hypocrisy, teaching, and tradition. Each of these concerns can be remedied by a firm commitment by the Church and by the individuals in the Church to *live the Word.*

The Hypocrisy Infection

What is the number-one perception of the Christian church today? No matter how you slice it, it always comes down to one word — hypocrisy. Hypocrisy has far more to do with honesty (including one's approach to the Bible itself) and transparency than it does being perfect. It insinuates that people say one thing (for example, we believe the Bible is God's Word), and live another way (for example, don't really believe all the Bible). It implies that people force their own legalism on others but are blind to their own faults and sins — even as they are very judgmental toward those who struggle with their own temptations.

In our study, hypocrisy is more important than the church being too political, irrelevant, or boring. Not coincidentally, 20-somethings who have never been to church at all voice the same criticism. David Kinnaman notes this in his book *Unchristian: What a New Generation*

Really Thinks about Christianity . . . and Why It Matters.[3] In part, he discovered these perceptions:

1. Christians say one thing but live something entirely different.

2. Christians are insincere and concerned only with converting others.

3. Christians show contempt for gays and lesbians.

4. Christians are boring, unintelligent, old-fashioned, and out of touch with reality.

5. Christians are primarily motivated by a political agenda and promote right-wing politics.

6. Christians are prideful and quick to find fault in others.

We have to admit that there is an element of truth in many of these critical perceptions. Certainly, the Church is often falsely judged for things that it does not do and does not believe. If you look through that list, however, isn't part of the problem that individual Christians and the Church as a whole do not live (or really believe) what the Bible says? The LifeWay study discovered similar concerns. Fifty-eight percent of Church dropouts in their study selected at least one church- or pastor-related reason for leaving church. Most common was, "church members seemed judgmental or hypocritical" (26 percent). Another 20 percent "didn't feel connected to the people in my church." The final category of reasons, "religious, ethical, or political beliefs," contributed to the departure of 52 percent of church dropouts.[4]

I greatly suspect (as I have observed this myself) that part of the problem is that many see those in the Church who are against

---

3. David Kinnaman, *Unchristian: What a New Generation Really Thinks about Christianity* (Grand Rapids, MI: Baker Books, 2007).

4. http://www.lifeway.com/lwc/article_main_page/0,1703,A%253D165951%2526 M%253D201117,00.html.

gay marriage and other aberrant lifestyles coming across as hating homosexuals. Most Christians don't teach that marriage is founded in Genesis, and it is God's Word that speaks against gay marriage. It is not our opinion we are imposing on people. People need to see Christians building their thinking consistently on God's Word, beginning in Genesis, to understand where our worldview comes from. Sadly, many Christians just impose their Christian morality from the top down, and this causes major problems.

Irrelevant Messages

I will get into this more in the next chapter, but I firmly believe that one of the reasons people aren't living by the Word is that they aren't being taught the Word. And certainly, because there is currently so much compromise of history in Genesis, church people by and large just do not understand that the Bible has to be the foundation for all of our thinking. When church people (remember the Sunday school problem) are brought up to allow millions of years and evolutionary ideas to be added into Scripture, many consciously or unconsciously take fallible ideas to Scripture — instead of using Scripture as a foundation for their thinking. Thus their worldview becomes a mixture of biblical morality and human opinion.

Remember, these kids in our sample were in church almost every Sunday. But they heard the same old stuff — shallow, relational, and sentimental stuff that doesn't have meat and substance and doesn't really connect them to reality. Many pastors strive to give entertaining messages that leave the congregation feeling inspired. But unless these messages are based on the inspired Word of God, those feelings will quickly fade away. Christianity without the Bible is a nebulous, lofty religion that doesn't connect to anything in the real world.

After speaking in a church about connecting the Bible to the real world — teaching clearly that the history in Genesis is true and why the gospel based in Genesis is true — a mother and her teenage daughter came up to me. (I have had many similar encounters over the years.) The mother said, "I can't thank you enough. I have been struggling to get my teenage daughter to church. She keeps telling me it is a waste of time and it's not relevant. We've had major problems. But this morning, she sat on the edge of her seat listening to every word you spoke, and after you finished she told me that for the first time she now understands what church is all about — for the first time she understands why Christianity is relevant. You really connected the dots for her this morning."

I spoke to the woman's daughter at length to glean why she reacted in such a way, and I believe she represents the feelings of the majority of church kids. She didn't see the Bible as real — it didn't connect to the real world. She thought church was just about spiritual stuff — but school was about real stuff. She was tired of the same old stories she had heard since Sunday school. She thought what she was taught at school showed the Bible couldn't be true — and no one at home or church could give her answers to her questions. Her mum told me she didn't have a clue what to say about dinosaurs and science issues, and she had just told her daughter it didn't matter, but come to church and trust Jesus anyway! But such a situation is repeated over and over and over again in the Church, and it is not being dealt with.

Why aren't the believers coming to church? When the Church no longer speaks to them, it becomes less relevant; the Church becomes like a clanging gong — making noise but offering nothing of practical value for their lives in the real world.

I believe that those in the pulpit are also missing the opportunity to preach about the relevancy of the Church itself. What does the Bible say about how we are to function together as a Body? Why is it important that we do not forsake our gathering together? The average person sitting in the pew probably doesn't know these things . . . and those who are already gone certainly don't understand that enough to reconnect themselves with a vibrant body of Bible-believing people.

The Tradition Trap

Conservative evangelical churches pride themselves on doing things "by the Book." But is that really the case? When we consider what "church" is from a *biblical* perspective, we must seriously and honestly ask the question, *Are our churches built on the Word of God or the wisdom of man?* In the Western world, when you say "church," at least four things immediately come to mind: a building, an order of service, sermons/Sunday school, and musical worship. That's biblical "church," right? You tell me! How many of these "church" things are found in Scripture? How many of them are man-made traditions?[5]

A Building?

There is not a single place in the New Testament where the term "church" refers to a building — not one! It wasn't until A.D. 190 that Clement of Alexandria referred to a meeting place as a "church." He was also the first person to use the phrase "go to church."[6] Every single one of the appearances of the word *ecclesia* in the New Testament refers to *a gathering or network of believers in Christ, not a physical structure or place.*

An "Order of Service"?

Virtually every evangelical Christian service follows the same basic format for "church" every time we meet. In its most basic form, we have *opening prayer and music, the sermon, and the closing song and/or prayer.* Beyond that, most local churches have a very distinct format that also includes announcements, an offering, and (at predetermined times) "communion." Strange, but you can look through the entire New Testament and find no such order, nor any suggestion that Christian gatherings should follow such an order. That doesn't mean that the order of worship we use is wrong; we just have to be honest and say that there's nothing biblical about it at all . . . and yet it's one of the most important aspects of our modern definition of "church."

---

5. We are indebted to the research of Frank Viola and George Barna presented in the book *Pagan Christianity? Exploring the Roots of Our Church Practices* (Carol Stream, IL: BarnaBooks, 2007). While we don't necessarily affirm their applications, their exploration of the roots of our modern church practices is illuminating and very thought provoking.
6. Clement of Alexandria, *The Instructor,* Book 3, chapter 11.

Sermons and Sunday School?

In the Bible, the good news was obviously preached to the unbelieving masses (Acts 2; Matthew 6–7). Doctrine was shared through
letters and taught in interactive small groups. By the fourth century, the
"Church" had adopted a format for teaching where a single man stood
in front of a passive audience and lectured.[7] This *can* still be a very useful format for teaching and preaching today, but it doesn't appear to
be the format that was used in the first-century Church where teaching believers was done in an interactive small group setting. (Again,
that doesn't mean that sermons are wrong; you just have to admit that
they're part of our man-made tradition, and not biblical history.)

The same goes for Sunday school. Sunday school didn't appear
on the scene until 1700 years after Christ. Robert Raikes of England
gets the credit for starting the first Sunday school in 1780.[8] Again, I'm
not saying that there's anything wrong with the idea of Sunday school
(even though it's really not working right now), but you're not going
to find it in the Bible; it's not a biblical element of "church." So then, if
your Sunday school isn't working like it should, why not do something
different!? I'm not saying you *should* do away with it (as we have stated
earlier, we advocate major radical changes), but I am saying that you
definitely *could* cancel your Sunday school program and not violate
any specific example in Scripture.

Worship Music?

I have spoken in hundreds of different churches, and some sort
of music is almost always included. I know that music can be a valid
form of worship, and I love great God-honoring, worshipful music.
Some claim church choirs were borrowed from Greek dramas and
were used to accommodate pagan worship.[9] But choirs are men-

---

7. Edwin Hatch, *Influence of Greek Ideas and Usages* (London, Edinburgh: Wil-
liams and Norgate, 1891), p. 119.
8. Iris V. Cully and Kendig Brubaker Cully, *Harper's Encyclopedia of Religious Education* (New York: HarperCollins Publishers, 1990), p. 625.
9. H.W. Parke, *The Oracles of Apollo in Asia Minor*, (London; Dover, NH: Croom
Helm, 1985), p. 102–103.

tioned in the Bible and were in existence before, during and after the Temple in the Old Testament. However, the point is Scripture does not mandate we have choirs.

In many evangelical churches, the choir has been replaced by a worship team who leads concert-style music and takes a considerable amount of the service time. Yes, music has a rich history in the Bible, but the *type* of worship that dominates and controls so much of "church" cannot be found in the New Testament . . . at all. I am only saying this to make a point that we don't have to do things just because it is tradition. As someone once said to me, "Do you know the seven last words of the Church? — we've never done it this way before!" And just because a church does something a different way doesn't mean everyone else has to follow!

If people want to make music the focal point of their service, they can — and many do. But the music is not really feeding the souls and protecting the minds of the congregation. Our statistics certainly show that music isn't the reason our young adults are leaving, and it's not the reason that they will come back. And again, we are not saying music is wrong — it is all a matter of what the focus and priority really should be.

Are we doing church "by the Book"? Just because we might be "conservative" or "traditional" doesn't mean that we are "biblical." It's safe to conclude that if one of the original Apostles visited one of our churches today, he wouldn't have any sort of clue that he was in a Christian gathering (unless he could understand our language). "Church" today is mostly driven by man-made traditions and not by the biblical mandates to defend the Word of God and live by the Word of God.

Many churches are waking up to this fact. Willow Creek (well-known for its seeker-sensitive approach to bring in people) recently had a look at what they were doing. Through a scientific survey like the one we conducted, they wanted to see if their church was really helping people grow. The findings shocked them:

We discovered that high levels of church activity *did not* predict increasing love for God or increasing love for other people. Now don't misread this! This does not mean that people highly involved in church activities don't love God. It simply means that they did not express a greater love for God than people who are less involved in church activities. In other words, an increasing level of activities did not *predict* an increase in love for God. Church activity alone made no direct impact on growing the heart . . . it was a flat line — and a stunning discovery for us.[10]

That is a tough pill to swallow. But at least they were willing to evaluate the effectiveness of what they are doing and consider making adjustments. Whether or not they make the right adjustments is another matter, of course.

When it comes to the modern-day church, I think one of the most piercing passages of Scripture is this:

They worship me in vain; their teachings are but rules taught by men. You have let go of the commands of God and are holding on to the traditions of men (Mark 7:6–8; NIV).

May we never hold to man-made religious traditions at the expense of defending God's Word and living God's Word. When it comes to "doing church," are we relying on man's wisdom or God's Word? If the forms and traditions that we use are working, then fine. But if they aren't working, we have a responsibility as well as the freedom to change what we are doing, provided that as a Church we do not neglect the commandments of God and worship God in vain.

---

10. Greg L. Hawkins and Cally Parkinson, *Reveal: Where Are You?* (South Barrington, IL: Willow, 2006), p. 35–36.

Rediscovering "Church"

Church can be defined many ways. It could be simply defined as *a group of individuals that prioritize the sharing of the Word of God and live by the principles of the Word of God.*

In order to stay true to such a definition, however, we must study God's Word to find out what the basic principles of "church" are! My challenge to you at this point is to *study for yourself* the principles and priorities of church in the New Testament.

Can I ask how you would define "church"? Is your definition based on man's thinking and tradition or God's Word? This is a critical, fundamental question. Yes, we are concerned about the exodus of young adults from the Church. But unless we know what the Bible means by "church," all of our efforts and concerns might be misguided. We need to be willing to question *all* assumptions that we have about "church" and let the Bible speak for itself when it talks about the Body of Christ.

The Greek word for "church" in the New Testament is *ecclesia*. It is used:

- 103 times in the New Testament;

- 20 times to refer to the universal Church;

- 34 times to refer to a group of churches;

- 49 times to refer to a specific local church.

I challenge you to take God at His Word and study both what the Bible says about Church *and* what it doesn't say. In order to see a glimpse of the Church in the first century, we must look at passages like Acts 2:42–47:

> They were continually devoting themselves to the apostles' teaching and to fellowship, to the breaking of bread and to prayer. Everyone kept feeling a sense of awe; and many

wonders and signs were taking place through the apostles. And all those who had believed were together and had all things in common; and they began selling their property and possessions and were sharing them with all, as anyone might have need. Day by day continuing with one mind in the temple, and breaking bread from house to house, they were taking their meals together with gladness and sincerity of heart, praising God and having favor with all the people. And the Lord was adding to their number day by day those who were being saved.

Descriptions like these give us a picture of what church is supposed to be all about: a community of people whose lives are empowered, directed, and energized by personal interaction with the Word of God and with each other. While some of the descriptions of the early Church are clearly cultural, many of them are universal as we discover the role of teachers, elders, deacons, and pastors — which also means there is structure as well as rules to abide by (for example, for disciplining when necessary). By connecting with what the Bible says about the Church, our churches connect with reality and regain the relevance that has been lost because we have focused only on our man-made traditions.

A very interesting New Testament study begins with a search of the words "one another." If you don't have a Bible study program on your computer, go to any of the online Bible search engines and type in those two words. You'll discover an amazing assortment of verses that describe what God really intended for lives to be like together as part of the Church.

A similar search can be made for the word "church." Read these passages and ask yourself, *Is this what "church" means to me? Do our traditions help us to be more like this kind of church or do they distract from the principles of the New Testament?* When you find clear principles and examples, pursue them with all your heart. If you don't find support for an aspect of "church" that you are used to or that you feel is being treated like a doctrine, know that it's only tradition. That doesn't mean that the tradition is necessarily bad. *Some traditions need to be kept, others are optional, and some need changing!*

One of the foundational biblical concepts for church is that we are to be a "body." Christianity is not a solo journey. How can you be a solid Christian in isolation? If you're in isolation, it means you're susceptible to the devil, evil, and you're not being held up by fellow believers. It's a rough world out there. We were not designed to go it alone. You might attend large worship services, but if you don't have those personal connections with the other members of the body, you're probably going to fall apart, because there's no one else there to help hold you together.

Unfortunately, the typical church does not provide these types of relationships or relevant teaching to their young adults. The Barna research indicates this trend:

> Much of the activity of young adults, such as it is, takes place outside congregations. Young adults were just as likely as older Americans to attend special worship events not sponsored by a local church, to participate in a spiritually oriented small group at work, to have a conversation with someone else who holds them accountable for living faith principles, and to attend a house church not associated with a conventional church. Interestingly, there was one area in which the spiritual activities of twentysomethings outpaced their predecessors: visiting faith-related websites.[11]

Because much of the conventional Church is neither defending the Word of God nor living by the Word of God, the young people who have left the Church — particularly those who still have strong levels of biblical belief — are trying to find it elsewhere. Very few are searching the Scriptures to discover what "church" is really supposed to be all about. All they know is that they're not finding it within the buildings

---

11. www.barna.org.

they grew up in, and they are willing to break with tradition to find it
— even when it looks nothing like the church of their parents. Right or
wrong, they are redefining what "church" means to their generation. I
personally believe this is part of the reason why movements are arising
in the Church that are not biblical in their beliefs but seem somewhat
attractive on the outside and seem to be more "loving" and "gentle"
and "caring." But in the long run, these churches have no real foundation — no real substance.

A Virtual Church?

Walt Wilson was a sales manager at Fairchild Semiconductor, a
start-up executive at Apple Computer, and a Silicon Valley business-
man. Now he is the chairman of Global Media Outreach, a ministry
that is trying to help the Church enter the digital age:

> The business term to describe the shift from atoms to bits is
> called *radical discontinuity*. Basically, it is change that happens
> so fast that we don't know how to describe it or even forecast
> it. It would be a huge mistake to think the Church is immune
> to this development. It is not. Many seekers across the world
> have shifted to information on the Internet instead of going to
> a place called church. People are looking for God in the world
> of bits, not atoms.[12] The Internet is now becoming the funnel
> *into* the church. If you are not using the Internet to conduct
> real ministry, then you don't exist to the current generation of
> seekers — two million daily![13]

Home Churches?

Sensing that the conventional church has dropped the ball when
it comes to defending God's Word and living God's Word, scores of
believers are leaving the pews and heading for the couches of living

---

12. If you'd like to be a part of reaching the millions of people who are searching
    the Internet to find Christ, contact Global Media Outreach and become one of
    their virtual missionaries.
13. http://www.lausanneworldpulse.com/perspectives.php/1043?pg=all.

rooms across the country. The resurgence in the "home church movement" has been significant. The home church has its advantages and disadvantages, just like every other form of church. Many people feel that this movement is a step backward and that home churches lack accountability, order, resources, and authority. Those who attend them argue that the Church survived and thrived for 300 years in homes before they started to meet in official church buildings. Home churches can also lack the biblical structure (as given clearly in Scripture) that includes elders, deacons, etc. Many of the young adults who go to them, however, feel like they have been "burned" by a traditional church that does not understand them. They argue that the environment is informal, with less liturgy, and highly interactive. They try to make it known that home churches are not just a place where a bunch of renegade lone rangers go to tie up their horses once in a while.

The Para-church as a Church?

For hundreds of years, concerned individuals have formed organizations that take up the slack where the traditional churches have been dropping the ball. Some print and distribute Bibles, some are mission organizations, and others target high school or college campuses. They refer to themselves as the "para-church" — but in many ways many of them become churches unto themselves. Many of these organizations excel at defending God's Word and living by God's Word. They often have "staff" people who are highly trained and serve as mature "pastors" to their flocks. Most members of the para-church are encouraged to also participate in a local church. Many of them do so, but to be honest, relevant "church" is taking place for them somewhere else.

Answers in Genesis is a para-church organization, but we believe it is very important to ensure people understand that we are not a church as such, just a specialist organization raised up to assist the Church in carrying out the Great Commission and building up the body of believers.

Healthy debate will undoubtedly continue about "alternative churches." Around the country, many conventional churches are beginning to realize they need to use the Bible as their primary "operator's manual" for church. Many of the committed believers who are leaving Church as we know it are honestly wrestling with all these new definitions. Many have concluded that Church is not something you go to; it's something you are. Many who are seeking to "live the Word" are even finding themselves back in traditional evangelical or liturgical churches. Things might even look the same on the outside, but with the Bible at the heart of all they do, everything feels different on the inside.

Not an Option

Hopefully, you have already seen that being part of a church is not optional for a committed believer in Jesus Christ (Heb. 10:25). Britt and I are praying that one of the consequences of this book is that churches will be changed from the inside out by the Word of God. We also pray that committed believers will have the freedom to leave, if necessary, to find *a group of individuals that prioritizes the sharing of the Word of God, teaching how to defend the Christian faith and uphold the authority of the Word in today's world, and lives by the principles of the Word of God.* And we are also praying that those who have left the Church will find their way back into this type of fellowship. Because of that, we asked those who are planning on returning to Church after they have kids a couple of important questions:

1. Do your closest friends attend church regularly right now? A full 50 percent said yes.

2. Have any of your friends invited you to go back to church with them? Sixty-one percent had been asked!

These numbers are actually encouraging (somewhat). At least half of the people who have left still have a tight connection with someone who is involved in a church. Hopefully these are good churches, too! Many of them have already been asked if they want to come home.

Only 27 percent of those who never go to church, however, have friends that attend church now. Yes, there is something to be said about positive peer pressure . . . even for adults. It still gives them a natural connection to the Church. Of those young people who expect to come back in the future, 61 percent of their friends invited them to church. And you might be that someone! Waggoner, who headed up the Life-Way survey, had this to say:

> Church leaders should passionately and consistently challenge church members to maximize their influence with youth and young adults. Frequent and intentional contact can either prevent or counteract the tendency of some to drop out of church. . . . This return to church after being gone for at least a year is primarily the result of encouragement from others. The most common reason for returning is "My parents or family members encouraged me to attend" (39 percent). Twenty-one percent attribute their return to "My friends or acquaintances encouraged me to attend." Combined, 50 percent of those who return were influenced by the encouragement of either family or friends. Young adults also return to church when they feel the desire personally or sense God calling them back: "I simply felt the desire to return" (34 percent) and "I felt that God was calling me to return to the church" (28 percent).[14]

And please, please remember that 30 percent of *all* the people who've left the Church "don't know" if they will be coming back or not. That's not just a statement of indecision; we should read that as a statement of *possibility*. In their hearts, they're still wondering. Perhaps all they need is someone to reach out to them in a real way, with real

14. http://www.lifeway.com/lwc/article_main_page/0,1703,A%253D165951%2526 M%253D201117,00.html.

information, living a real Christian life. When it comes to church, they are looking for the real deal. Perhaps you need only let them know that the door is still open and that they're still always welcome to come back and be a part of the Body.

The Most Important Thing

Churches that defend God's Word and live by God's Word can once again become "the real deal" to the generation of young adults that has left and the next generation that is teetering on the edge. But I strongly encourage you to always remember that a church is a group of individuals . . . and you are an individual. We hope that you might actually be an agent of change within the group, but in all honesty, the *only* thing you can really control is yourself — and, in fact, the *most important* thing you can control is *yourself*. It's so easy to point a judgmental (and hypocritical) finger at the Church and think, *Oh, if only they would live by the Word.* But what about you: are you living by the Word? It turns out that this is a vital question for you personally — far more important than whether or not you are attending church. After Willow Creek realized that what they were doing as a church was not helping people grow spiritually, they set out to find out what does help. Four years, 200 churches, and 80,000 surveys later, they found this:

> Everywhere we turned the data revealed the same truth: spending time in the Bible is hands down the highest impact personal spiritual practice. More specifically, "I reflect on the meaning of Scripture in my life" is the spiritual practice that is most predictive of growth. . . . Reflecting on Scripture implies a contemplative process, one of thoughtful and careful deliberation. This practice of "reflecting on the meaning of Scripture in my life" is about using God's Word as a mirror that reflects back the truth of Scripture on the actions, decisions, and defense of one's daily life. This is not about skimming through a Bible passage or devotional in a mechanical

way. This is a powerful experience of personal meditation that catalyzes spiritual growth, starting at the very beginning of the spiritual journey.[15]

Now how such a church responds to this, of course, is another matter. If they don't understand the issues as Britt's research has discovered, and if they don't take an uncompromising stand on Genesis, then we would say it would all be to no avail in the long run.

We do have to defend the word in this post-Christian culture, as we have outlined in previous chapters; we must make the connection between fact and faith so that the Scriptures again become authoritative and relevant in the Church and in the culture. The Willow Creek research shows that it wasn't their progressive musical worship, it wasn't their dynamic small groups, and it wasn't their seeker-sensitive (watered down) Sunday sermons. True spiritual growth and a healthy church all start with an individual — with you — accepting the Word of God for what it is — the absolute authority — and treating it accordingly. The Bible from Genesis to Revelation is the living Word of God. The written, uncompromised Word of God in your mind and the presence of the Holy Spirit of Christ in your heart is the pure essence of Christianity. When you gather together a group of people with that, "church happens." Jesus said:

> I am the vine, you are the branches; he who abides in Me and I in him, he bears much fruit, for apart from Me you can do nothing (John 15:5).

When writing about the profound and powerful mystery of being a Christian, Paul wrote:

> I can do all things through Him who strengthens me (Phil. 4:13).

---

15. Greg L. Hawkins and Cally Parkinson, *Follow Me: What's Next for You?* (South Barrington, IL: Willow, 2007), p. 114.

Are you specifically willing to commit to live an authentic Christian life, to "live the Word" as God empowers you through His Holy Spirit so that you can be "the real deal" with Christ, with yourself, with your family, with the Church, and with the world? Brit and I pray so.

> Long for the pure milk of the word, so that by it you might grow in respect to salvation (1 Pet. 2:2).

Britt's Bit: It's Hard to Explain Sometimes

Every once in a while, some numbers just don't make sense. It makes you wonder how much people have really thought through their Christian teachings and their Christian faith. Sometimes I have to push myself back from my desk, scratch my head a little bit, look up at the ceiling, and wonder *what in the world are these people thinking?*

Do you believe that dinosaurs died out before people were on the planet?

60% of those who attend church on Easter and Christmas said yes.

32% of those who don't attend church at all said yes.

This is exactly backward of what we would expect. In every other area of belief, those who attend church at the holidays gave more accurate biblical answers to our questions . . . except this one! It's sad but true that many Christians have not logically thought through the earlier teachings in their lives. I believe those who attend church only on Christmas or Easter and those who don't attend at all are answering the question about dinosaurs based more upon movies they've seen than scriptural teachings. Sometimes you just have to accept that people are not always logical and therefore are never predictable.

But this was the one that really got me wondering: *Do you believe that God used evolution to change one kind of animal to another?*

- 24% said yes.

When we asked the same group this question: *Do you believe that humans evolved from apelike ancestors?*

- 30% said yes.

You would expect to have the same identical answer to both of these questions. However, we don't. And the reason we don't have the same answer is that these young people were not adequately equipped when they were younger to understand and defend the Scriptures.

CHAPTER 7

Welcome to the Revolution

"Insanity" is doing the same thing over and over and expecting a different result. — Anonymous

Desperate times call for desperate measures — and these are desperate times. We *do* have an epidemic on our hands. Survey after survey has revealed that over 60 percent of the children who grow up in our churches will leave them as they reach the threshold of young adulthood. The empty and obsolete churches of England foreshadow the future in America. Where England is today, we will be tomorrow[1] — unless we take strategic action now. We don't need a remodel; we need a complete renovation. We don't need a Band-Aid; we need radical surgery. It's time for a revolution; it's time for a new Reformation in the Church — to call the Church back to the authority of the Word of God, beginning in Genesis.

---

1. It is true that recent surveys show certain churches such as Evangelical and Pentecostal are growing, but overall church attendance across all denominations is way down.

No, the numbers are not good. By surveying a thousand young adults who have left solid Bible-believing churches, we have gotten a much clearer profile of the lost generation. More sobering is the fact that the current Sunday school is doing very little (at best) and can even be significantly detrimental to the beliefs and the faith of the children we send there.

We have shown that those who leave the Church can be broken into two categories: Group 1, which never comes to church during the holidays and has no plans on returning to church after they have children. This group has serious doubts about the relevancy of Scripture. Group 2, on the other hand, comes to church on Easter or Christmas or both, and will likely return to the Church after they have children. They have a relatively high level of belief in biblical truth, but they find the Church to be irrelevant.

So what is to be done? We have already established that we need to *defend the Word* and we need to *live the Word*. What does this mean for the young adults who are already gone? David Kinnaman points out a sobering challenge:

> There is considerable debate about whether the disengagement of twentysomethings is a lifestage issue — that is, a predictable element in the progression of people's development as they go through various family, occupational, and chronological stages — or whether it is unique to this generation. While there is some truth to both explanations, this debate misses the point, which is that the current state of ministry to twentysomethings is woefully inadequate to address the spiritual needs of millions of young adults. These individuals are making significant life choices and determining the patterns and preferences of their spiritual reality while churches wait, generally in vain, for them to return after college or when the kids come. When and if young adults do return to churches, it is difficult to convince them that a passionate pursuit of

Christ is anything more than a nice add-on to their cluttered lifestyle.[2]

Strategic search and rescue efforts need to continue helping those who have wandered from the flock find their way back. Many times a sincere invitation from a friend is all it takes. But even if they agree to come back, unless the Church is standing on the authority of the Word of God in an uncompromising way, teaching them how to answer the skeptical questions of the age, and challenging them to build their thinking in every area on God's Word — they will probably not stay.

The obvious remaining question, however, is this: *How do we curb the epidemic in the flock that is still under our care — the high school, middle school, and elementary students who are still coming in almost every Sunday?*

We believe that a four-pronged approach is in order. Parents, Christian educators, youth pastors, and pastors all have a role to play in the solution. All of us in the Body are called to defend the Word and live the Word. Our specific mandates, however, are unique, and our strategic action points vary depending upon where God has placed us. And teaching creation and biblical apologetics is a necessary part for all!

To Parents

Your Call

Defend the Word.
Live the Word.

Your Mandate

Be diligent to present yourselves approved to God as a workman who does not need to be ashamed, accurately handling the word of truth (2 Tim. 2:15).

Southern Baptist Convention researcher Ed Stetzer noted:

---

2. David Kinneman, *Unchristian: What a New Generation Really Thinks about Christianity — and Why It Matters* (Grand Rapids, MI: Baker Books, 2007).

There is no easy way to say it, but it must be said. Parents and churches are not passing on a robust Christian faith and an accompanying commitment to the church. We can take some solace in the fact that many do eventually return. But, Christian parents and churches need to ask the hard question, "What is it about our faith commitment that does not find root in the lives of our children ?"[3]

That's not a rhetorical question. Why isn't our faith taking root in our children? First, it's possible that the parents themselves do not have a "robust Christian faith" to start with. Christianity is contagious, but children won't catch it unless the parents are infected. If your children aren't following Christ, you must first check to see if they're following your lead! Your first priority as a parent is to live the Word of God in a natural, sincere way. If you try to preach it to your kids without living it, you'll only add to the hypocrisy that turned so many of them away. Consider this challenge:

> Hear, O Israel! The LORD is our God, the LORD is one! You shall love the LORD your God with all your heart and with all your soul and with all your might. These words, which I am commanding you today, shall be on your heart. You shall teach them diligently to your sons and shall talk of them when you sit in your house and when you walk by the way and when you lie down and when you rise up. You shall bind them as a sign on your hand and they shall be as frontals on your forehead. You shall write them on the doorposts of your house and on your gates (Deut. 6:4–9).

Parent, it's time to search your own heart and know your own ways and see if there is any hurtful way within you (Ps. 139:24). Do you love the Lord our God with all your heart and with all your soul and with

---

3. http://www.lifeway.com/lwc/article_main_page/0,1703,A%253D165951%2526 M%253D201117,00.html.

all your might? Do you take the words of God and treasure them in your heart and teach them to your kids by talking to them about God's Word as if it's a normal part of your life? *Is* it your life? The faith of your family starts with you. The Barna Group explained it this way:

> It's not entirely surprising that deep, lasting spiritual trans-formation rarely happens among teenagers — it's hard work at any age, let alone with the distractions of youth. And, since teenagers' faith often mirrors the intensity of their parents', youth workers face steep challenges because they are trying to impart something of spiritual significance that teenagers generally do not receive from home.[4]

Second, you need to realize that our society is no longer "Christian." Our kids are living in a culture that is saturated with counter-Christian messages built on a foundation of evolutionary secular humanism. It's your job to protect your kids and prepare them for life in this post-Christian society. You need to teach them how to answer the skeptical questions of this age. Show them that you do not compromise God's Word with man's fallible word (for example, by allowing millions of years or evolutionary ideas to invade Scripture and thus undermine biblical authority).

It's not just an issue of homeschooling; it is an issue of true biblical home education. If our survey should teach you anything, it's that you can no longer depend on the Sunday school and youth ministries in your church to educate your kids in the things of God. In all honesty, this was never their responsibility in the first place. This is your job; this is your responsibility; you need to step up to the plate and take charge.

Action Points

- **Humble yourself before God: submit yourself to Him to be used as a tool in His hand for ministry in your own home**. The strength and power of your ministry

---

4. www.barnagroup.org.

must come from the presence of the Holy Spirit working through you according to the Word of God. Trying to do this by yourself, rather than allowing God to work through you as He chooses, will eventually lead to failure.

If you now realize you have compromised God's Word (for example, in Genesis), then ask the Lord to forgive you, and admit to your children you were wrong and then diligently teach them how to answer skeptical questions and not compromise God's Word. Let your children see you have a high view of Scripture as you should.

- **Make the Word of God a natural presence in your home.** Follow the command in Deuteronomy chapter 6 to talk about the Word with your kids and spouse. Write them down and post them in prominent places in your home. Ask God to create inside of you a love for Him that flows from your whole heart, mind, soul, and spirit. If you need to study up on how creation relates to the gospel and the rest of Scripture, then read Genesis 1–11, the Gospel of John, the Book of Romans, and the last two chapters of Revelation. This will give you a good overview to start with.

- **Evaluate your church.** Is your church defending the Word and living by the Word? Chances are you're going to have to make a decision to either stay as a committed agent of change, or leave and join a church that already shares your stand in these areas.

Whatever you do, don't punt your responsibilities to somebody else. God has placed you in your family for a reason. He will give you the strength and wisdom that you need to carry out your mandate — if you humble yourself before Him and allow Him to work through you.

For a list of recommended resources, see appendix 4.

To the Christian Educator

Your Call

Defend the Word.

Live the Word.

Your Mandate

Let not many of you become teachers, my brethren, knowing that as such we will incur a stricter judgment (James 3:1).

Christian educators — those of you who serve in Sunday schools
and elementary Christian schools — our hats go off to you for your
sincere devotion to this next generation. At the same time, we have to
make an honest evaluation of the effectiveness of your efforts. What
you are doing is not working as it should. It's not getting through and
it's not doing the job. We know you are in a key position to make major
changes in the lives of your students. You are the M*A*S*H unit on
the front lines of this disease. You are the nurses and the doctors that
are positioned to counter the epidemic, and you *must* begin to defend
the Word with your pupils at a very young age. You must teach them
how to defend themselves and the Word of God in a secular world and
show them how the Bible connects to the real world.

Students are not being taught how to defend their faith, how to
answer skeptical questions, how to answer the questions of this age
concerning the age of the earth/evolution, etc. We know that many of
you are handed pre-made lesson plans. We know that you probably
haven't been trained in how to teach apologetics yourselves. We know
that many of you may even be harboring doubts of your own. It doesn't
have to be that way.

Action Points

- **Humble yourself before God**. Ask for His guidance and
  place your dependence fully on Him to lead you and em-
  power you for the ministry that He entrusted to you. Shine

the light of God's Word into your heart and test whether you have stood on the Bible as the absolute authority, or whether you have compromised. The Lord forgives. Pray for the courage to take the stand you need to, always remembering:

> But whoever causes one of these little ones who believe in Me to stumble, it would be better for him to have a heavy millstone hung around his neck, and to be drowned in the depth of the sea (Matt. 18:6).

- **Make your own spiritual life a priority.** Far too often, faithful Christian educators are trying to feed their students when their own plate is empty. Take the time to pamper yourself spiritually. Read the Word for yourself. Prioritize nurturing times of prayer and meditation with the Lord. Study carefully the Word of God and allow the Holy Spirit to minister to your soul. Relevant books dealing with how to understand apologetics arguments for today's world, and how to logically argue the Christian faith against the skeptical questions of this era, are now available. Diligently prepare yourself for the task. Take care of yourself first and then God will work through you to take care of your students.

- **Take responsibility.** Your pastor is probably burned out and distracted with other things. Your Christian education director is probably relieved just to have you filling a spot in the program. But it's really God who's put you in this position, and you need to take full responsibility for what you're teaching and how you are teaching it. With sensitivity and determination you can also become a change agent in your program.

- **Get trained.** I know that most of you are volunteers, but you need to become pros. A tremendous amount of dynamic and encouraging training materials are available to you, no matter what your specific responsibility is in the Christian education system. Find a book; watch a DVD; go to a conference . . . your ministry will be the better because of it. Learn how to communicate to the age group you are dealing with.

- **Get armed to the hilt with solid curriculum.** With good materials, the devoted Christian educator becomes a very powerful influencer for truth. A lady who worked for a Christian publishing company that published Sunday school curricula once said to me, "You would love our Sunday school curricula. We teach the children that Genesis is true, and that there really was a global Flood. The students learn that Noah and the animals went on board the ark and came off the ark after the Flood. We make sure we tell the students this was a real event. Isn't that great?"

My response shocked her. I asked, "Tell me, did the curriculum actually teach the account of the Flood as real history — or just a story? Do you know one of the most asked questions concerning Noah and the ark? Did you explain how Noah could fit all the animals on the ark? [That is one of the skeptical comments of our day by which people claim the account of the Noah's ark cannot be true.] Tell me, did you connect the ark/Flood account to biology? Did you explain to them that Noah only took representative kinds of land animals on board the ark? [He would only need two of the dog kind, not all the dog varieties we see today; only two of the elephant kind; only two of the horse kind; two of the camel kind; and so on.] Did you teach them answers to the skeptical questions of the day to show them that they can defend the Christian faith against the skeptics of this age? Did you teach them from a perspective of apologetics, preparing them for the age they live in, for what they will be taught at school, for the skeptical questions about the Bible they will be confronted with — or did you just teach it to them as a *story*? Did you connect the Flood to the fossils? Did you prepare them for what they will hear on TV and at school concerning millions of years? Did you teach them that the fossils could not have been laid down millions of years before Adam sinned? Did you explain that the Flood makes sense of most of the fossil record? Did you connect the Flood to geology . . . or did you just teach the account as a *story*?"

These are just some of the questions in relation to the topic of the Flood and Noah's ark — but one would have to do much the same sort of thing with every topic. In other words, for each subject:

1. Define the skeptical questions of this age that are leveled against this particular account from the Bible.

2. Teach students how to answer these questions.

3. Find ways we can connect this account with the real world; for example, archaeology, biology, anthropology, astronomy, and geology.

4. Explore the practical application that can be made.

5. Ensure students understand historical events as real history, doctrine, etc., from this passage.

6. Explain to students how it all relates to biblical authority and the gospel.

7. Where possible, connect the topic back to Genesis — you may be surprised at how easy this will come to you once you begin to do it.

- **Teach Bible history, not Bible stories**. The point is, most Sunday school material just teaches stories! Most Sunday school teachers don't know how to answer the skeptical questions of the day. Sunday school is not preparing the children for what they will be taught at school; it is not preparing them to be able to defend the Christian faith. Most curricula ignores apologetics and just teaches (maybe in a more contemporary way perhaps) basic Bible stories — spiritual and moral matters. Most such teaching does not connect the Bible to the real world. And sadly, in most instances, children are either actively told to believe what they are taught at school, or by default, they are led to believe that this is what they must do.

Often those kids who attend Sunday school will ask their Sunday school teachers (or pastors and/or parents) about millions of years, or dinosaurs and associated topics, wanting an answer from an authority figure who represents, in their eyes, Christianity and the Bible. And what do they hear?

Sadly, in the majority of instances, the Sunday school teachers will tell them that that is not a topic for Sunday school/church — and/or just believe the Bible regardless — and/or they can believe in millions of years and evolution as long as they trust in Jesus. The most important thing as far as the teacher is concerned is that the students trust in Jesus — those questions the students asked about origins issues aren't that important. It doesn't matter what one believes about Genesis.

Not only do I know this from years of experience in the biblical creation apologetics ministry, but it is obvious from the plethora of Sunday school curricula, Bible study and youth curricula, and children's books. Most such resources either allow for millions of years of evolution, or just teach the Genesis account as Bible stories, not dealing with issues of the fossils, the age of the earth, and associated topics. Or they teach that there are different views on Genesis and it doesn't matter what one believes, or they ignore Genesis altogether.

And by the way, the word "story" actually means "fairy tale" — and in today's world, most people really do think "fairy tale" when they hear the word "story." We have got to stop telling kids today we are going to read them or teach them a "Bible story." We have to use different terms like "this *account* of . . ." or something similar to help them understand this is *real* history.

Remember, one of your major objectives is to help students make a link between their faith and fact. That's going to require that you bring historical (and observational) science back into the Church and back into your Sunday schools. You *can* help your students make a connection between the Bible and reality. Whatever you do, don't teach Bible "stories." Teach Bible *history*. Use real maps, real artifacts, and real illustrations of what really happened. Most of the pictures we present to our children look like cartoon fairy tales. Even the pictures that we present of Noah's ark make it look like an overgrown bathtub with animals' heads sticking out of the windows. We are not presenting Noah's ark as it really might have looked. We aren't making it look like a real boat. Make it as real as it really was.

For a list of recommended resources, see appendix 5.

To the Youth Pastor

Your Call

Defend the Word.
Live the Word.

Your Mandate

Train up a child in the way he should go, even when he is old he will not depart from it (Prov. 22:6).

Still, one of the most striking findings from the research is the broad base of opportunities that Christian churches in America have to work with teenagers. Overall, more than four out of five teens say they have attended a church for a period of at least two months during their teenage years (81%). This represents substantial penetration and significant prospects for influencing the nation's 24 million teens. —Barna Research.[5]

---

5. www.barna.org/...teensnext.../147-most-twentysomethings-put-christianity-on-the-shelf-following-spiritually-active-teen-years.

Those of you who work with teenagers are standing at the threshold of adulthood for teenagers who have grown up in the Church. Think about that for a moment. They are about to step out that door of the church, and approximately 60 percent of them will not come back after they leave your ministry. Are your students already gone? Kinnaman suggests a new test for a "successful" teen ministry:

> Much of the ministry to teenagers in America needs an overhaul — not because churches fail to attract significant numbers of young people, but because so much of those efforts are not creating a sustainable faith beyond high school. There are certainly effective youth ministries across the country, but the levels of disengagement among twentysomethings suggest that youth ministry fails too often at discipleship and faith formation. A new standard for viable youth ministry should be — not the number of attendees, the sophistication of the events, or the "cool" factor of the youth group — but whether teens have the commitment, passion, and resources to pursue Christ intentionally and wholeheartedly after they leave the youth ministry nest.[6]

That's probably something you don't get a chance to think about much. Many of you are fresh out of college and are thrust into churches that expect you to implement a "get them to come no matter what" approach. You're being paid to bring kids in and to keep them occupied. Fun, music, and entertainment can quickly become the focus of your creativity. (Defending the Word and living the Word become secondary priorities.) You have more to offer than that. You're strategically placed during a strategic time of life, and you can make a powerful difference that lasts a lifetime if you're willing to look past your attendance figures on a Wednesday night.

Action Points

- **Get on your knees and recommit yourself to effective ministry.** You may have to repent for trying to seek the approval

---

6. Ibid.

of other people rather than doing what you know God has called you to do. You may have to ask for forgiveness for compromising the Word of God in order to make your ministry attractive and fun for your students. Repent of all that, and ask God to lead you in a new and everlasting way.

- **Equip your parents.** This might be the most important thing you can do. Make "parental training" part of your job description and then go for it. I know this isn't a new thought, but how many youth pastors actually prioritize this type of strategic ministry? Work in conjunction with your Christian educators so that you can raise up an army of parents who can disciple and train their own kids from the cradle to graduation.

- **Develop teenagers' abilities to contemplate and develop their own personal worldview.** Most likely, your students are already being bombarded with secular influences. You can teach them how to defend the Word, and how to live the Word in an antagonistic, anti-Christian world.

For a list of recommended resources, see appendix 6.

To the Pastor

Your Call

Defend the Word.
Live the Word.

Your Mandate

I solemnly charge you in the presence of God and of Christ Jesus, who is to judge the living and the dead, and by His appearing and His Kingdom: preach the word; be ready in season and out of season; reprove, rebuke, exhort, with great patience and instruction. For the time will come when they will not endure sound doctrine; but wanting to have their ears tickled, they will accumulate for themselves teachers in accordance to their own desires, and will turn away their ears from the truth and will turn aside to myths (2 Tim. 4:1–4).

For the equipping of the saints for the work of service, to the building up of the body of Christ; until we all attain to the unity of the faith, and of the knowledge of the Son of God (Eph. 4:12–13).

Okay, pastors, now it's your turn. Its inventory time; it's honesty time. It's time to look inside your heart and inside your church and let God do a surprise inspection so you can face the statistical facts that came out of this study. Perhaps your church is one of the rare exceptions, but if it's not, you need to wake up and smell the coffee. You must be willing to suck up your pride and take some responsibility. *Two out of three of the teenagers who grew up in your church are already gone.* Is that "just the way it is," or is there something you can, should, and must be doing? Ask yourself these important questions:

1. Am I preaching the Word of God?

2. Am I defending the Word of God?

3. Am I and my church living the Word of God or am I perpetuating a religious institution that is trapped in tradition?

4. Have I compromised the Word, particularly in Genesis, and unwittingly undermined biblical authority to those who are already gone and those who will go?

5. Have I ensured that all the teaching curricula in the various church programs really is reaching the kids and parents where they are today? Is it just reaching the "Jew" or is it reaching the "Grecks"?

6. Have I allowed a philosophy to make the church look more like the world to try to attract people, instead of teaching relevant answers the world needs?

7. Is music the priority in the church or is teaching the Word the priority?

The answer to the first question might surprise you. After all the churches that he has surveyed, Britt believes that, if you're lucky, 20 percent of your congregation walks away feeling spiritually uplifted on a given Sunday morning. Let's face it: most people are tired of milk-toast messages. They want the real thing; they want to hear from the Scriptures that are living and active and sharper than any two-edged sword. The temptation is to back off the meat and potatoes and feed them sugar and spice — something that is exciting, dynamic, and entertaining. That might hold them for the moment, but in the long run it sacrifices your relevancy. People get bored; they wish for something that connects to the real world . . . and they fade away even more. When they come to your church hungry on a Sunday morning, do you give them a healthy dose of meat? Or do they only walk away with a temporary sweet taste on their tongue that will not last past noon?

All week long, those who attend your church are bombarded in their workplace and in the media by messages that undermine the authority of God's Word, particularly the Genesis accounts. Do you regularly defend God's Word from the pulpit? Have you equipped those sitting in the pews to give an answer for the hope that is in them? This is something that must be done. You may need to get out of your little Christian bubble for a while to understand what we are really talking about. Sit in a fast-food restaurant at lunchtime and listen to the high school students talking. Go stand by the water cooler in the break room of a major corporation and listen to the talk of the secretaries during break. It's a rough world out there. The people who come to find some rest and relief on Sunday are fighting a major battle against ungodly influences the other six days of the week. Are you giving them what they need to survive and thrive in the world? Have you ever really sat down with the young people and asked them questions to see at what point they are, what they really believe, and what the stumbling blocks are to their faith? You will find (if you ask the right questions) that millions of years and questions about science and Genesis are major issues with them.

And, have you become a slave to man-made religious traditions that are imprisoning your congregation and dictating your ministry? I think there's a good chance that you have . . . and I am so, so sorry about that. Countless pastors begin their ministry with the hope and the expectation that they will be a part of an authentic body of believers who experience the simplicity and purity of devotion to Christ. But usually the pastors themselves become casualties of burnout from man-made religious institutions that place huge burdens and expectations on their leaders. That's reality, but thankfully there are things that you can do about it.

Action Points

- **Reevaluate your call.** The demands on you as a pastor can quickly destroy your vision and purpose in ministry. I would challenge you to back off a little bit and rethink who you are, what you are doing, and why you are doing it. It might be time to dust off those distant dreams you had for vibrant ministry back in seminary. It might be time for a sabbatical. It is definitely time to make some radical changes in the way you do church.

- **Simplify and clarify your objectives.** Your primary call is to defend God's Word and live by God's Word. Your mandate is to preach the Word and to equip others to minister and live by the Word. It might be time to take a day or two and get away with a blank legal pad and your Bible and rethink what that means for you and your church. Are you just teaching about heavenly things — relationships, spiritual, and moral things? Have you ignored the "earthly things"?

- **Draw some lines in the sand.** If your ministry is driven by denominational and congregational expectations rather than Scripture, any changes that you make will expose you to pressure and complaint from those who feel safe with the status quo. It's likely that a certain faction within your church will think it's time for you to leave. You will likely need to draw some lines in the sand and say, "God's taking us in a new direction here. If you don't like it, it might be time for *you* to leave." Only you can decide whether or not it's worth the fight, but let me tell you that I've visited thousands of churches and I know that there *are* some things worth fighting for, and a vibrant new vision for unleashing God's Word in the local church is always preferable to a slow, draining, inevitable death of a congregation that is stuck in its old ways. You're likely to lose some people. But don't worry; chances are there is another irrelevant, anemic church building with plenty of empty pews just down the block. Give them the freedom to take the hike.

And if you do take a strong stand on Genesis, and accept no compromise, and begin teaching creation and general biblical apologetics, you will most likely receive complaints. Certain people who have compromised on these issues themselves (maybe a scientist, or teacher, or doctor) will say they will leave if you continue with such things. There will be pressure regarding financial support for the church — but what is more important? Isn't the priority the authority of Scripture and the teaching of the Word? God wants us to be faithful to the Word.

- **Defend the Word.** If you haven't taught good apologetics to your church, if you haven't equipped your Christian educators to do the same, you're in for a wonderful surprise: people love this stuff! It affirms their faith; it emboldens their witness; it helps them make a tangible connection between faith and fact. As many have said to us, "This makes the Bible so real!" Apologetics is one of the most life-giving things that you can inject into the veins of your church. A regular injection of Bible-defending, faith-affirming scientific and historical evidence will add new life to both you and your congregation. Don't hold back. They really want to have answers to the questions that cause them to doubt.

- **Teach the Word.** People want meat; they want something that is relevant; they want the Word of God. You need to understand that, and you are responsible for that. Period. Sure, you might lose some people who don't really believe the Bible in the first place, but you know what? You might as well speed up the process, because they are already gone.

- **Teach about the Word.** People want to know that "Jesus loves me." But quite frankly, because "the Bible tells me so" isn't going to be enough anymore. Before people will see the Bible as relevant, you need to teach them that it is authoritative and accurate. For example, does your congregation know what it means that the Bible is "inspired by God"? Some of our survey results would indicate that many people weren't even sure what that means. Many seem to think that that meant that the Bible was "inspirational," because many of them indicated that they believe the words of the Bible came from the wisdom of men and not from the declaration of God. You need to communicate to them what it means when we say that the Bible is "God breathed." They need general Bible apologetics as well as sound exegetical teaching.

- **Teach about the Church.** Our survey showed that 38 percent of the people who have left the Church still believe that the Bible is true, and yet the Church is not relevant enough to them to get them out of bed on Sunday morning. This reflects the failure of the Church to excite their young people by breathing life into the Scriptures. Christians need fellowship of other Christians in order to be able to grow spiritually and to be taught about Christian life. Too often, these young people view the Church through the hypocrisy of the Church leaders, and thus ignore those leaders' teachings.

- **Back off on the entertainment factor.** I recognize that you pastors are dealing with a number of different pressures. Fiscal responsibilities can place tremendous expectations upon you to bring in new people quickly and keep the ones that you have. The temptation is to go for the easy fix and focus on creating a church experience that is exciting, dynamic, and entertaining. Far too often this is done at the expense of legitimate community and the preaching of God's Word. What is the long-term result of a short-term fix? You sacrifice your relevancy. Because you're only feeding them sweet things that tickle their tongues, their hunger is rarely satisfied. They quickly come back expecting another bigger and better sugar fix. Deep inside, however, they really want some meat. And yet what do you do to keep their attention? You make your message even shorter and even more entertaining. Usually the emphasis turns more toward music, but that's a mistake. (Only 1 percent of the 1,000 young adults that we surveyed left the Church because of the music. A significant portion of those who left reported that they really did miss the preaching of God's Word.) Pretty soon this starts to spiral downward until you really are communicating nothing of substance and the Bible takes the back shelf in the church service.

- **Pass the torch**. Rather than just hoping the teenagers are going to come back after they graduate, why not put them in charge? Let's be honest, there are many things that we can do to make our churches more culturally relevant to the 20-something generation. Nobody knows how to do this more intuitively than they do. I would highly recommend commissioning a group of trusted elders who will walk alongside teens and mentor, disciple, and equip them to be unleashed in ministry to their own generation. While never compromising Scripture, they just might totally re-invent what "church" looks like for the upcoming genera-tion. They will no doubt need training in apologetics so they can pass that information on.

Yes, desperate times require desperate actions. And the situation in the Church today, as we have shown, is critical and its future impact is at great risk. The exciting thing is that the decisions and commitment of a few can begin the healing process that stops the epidemic and infuses new life and vitality into the lives of 20-somethings and those who will follow in their footsteps. Parents, Christian educators, youth pastors, and pastors hold in their hands the medicine that can bring the cure to this spreading epidemic of apathy and disengagement.

One thousand 20-somethings have revealed the answer. They have shared why they have walked away. We now know what we can do. There is a solution. The question is now one of commitment to the "cure."

Are you willing to administer the "medicine" to those who need it so desperately?

For a list of recommended resources, see appendix 7.

Final Thoughts

Britain has lost its Christian soul. In this post-Christendom Britain, we cannot afford to neglect prayerful and spirit-led strat-egies for long-term change, for there is much work to be done.

— The Rev. Joel Edwards,
head of the Evangelical Alliance in England[7]

Recently I was made aware of another collection of photos of churches that had become "redundant" — useless leftovers that were not needed to fulfill their intended purpose.

---

7. 2005 Evangelical Alliance, http://www.eauk.org/resources/info/statistics/2005 englishchurchcensus.cfm.

A former Methodist church built in 1839 now houses the Historical Society of Amherst, New Hampshire.

A church building now serving as a business, Cabinet Press, located in Milford, New Hampshire.

A church facility in Milford, New Hampshire, that is now the home of Musical Instrument String Superstore.

Master An's Martial Arts College in Bedford, New Hampshire.

Repurposed church building which is the Town Hall of Auburn, New Hampshire

There's just one major difference between these churches and the ones we contemplated at the beginning of this book: these churches are not in England. They are in New England. As England is, so we will be if we don't take strategic action now. American Christianity could be on the edge of obsolescence in less than two generations. The epidemic is continuing to spread and will do so unless something is done.

But may I leave you with a different kind of vision? Consider the possibilities of a revolution, a reformation, and a renovation of church as we know it in America today. What if our churches were to truly become gatherings of individuals who defend God's Word and live by God's Word? Imagine the potential as millions of Bible-believing Christians in this country evaluate their own lives, their own families, their own churches, and their own country, and begin to strategically do their part by allowing God to use them in any way that He sees fit to protect the vital Body of Christ and to reach out to those who have left her and those who meet her.

Throughout human history, the course of human events has been turned many, many times by those who see what is, who see what is coming, and who lay down their lives to alter the course of the future for the betterment of all. Our country has forsaken its Christian soul. We need to see that for what it is and take action in prayerful and biblically based strategies.

Again, we call for a new reformation. In a sense (symbolically), we need to be nailing Genesis 1–11 on the doors of churches (akin to what Martin Luther did), seminaries, and Christian and Bible colleges, to call the Church back to the authority of the Word of God. In this era of history, we really "lost" that authority beginning in Genesis; that is where we need to reestablish it. When the Church gets back to the authority of the Word of God, then it can be the salt and light to influence the culture with God's Word to change hearts and minds — and consequently change the culture.

Martin Luther is purported to have stated:

If I profess with the loudest voice and clearest exposition every portion of the Word of God except precisely that little point which the world and the devil are at that moment attacking, I am not confessing Christ, however boldly I may be professing Him. Where the battle rages there the loyalty of the soldier is proved; and to be steady on all the battle front besides, is mere flight and disgrace if he flinches at that point.[8]

May the Lord bless you and keep you, may He cause His face to shine upon you and give you strength. Regardless of what the future holds for us, our families, our church, and our world, may we have the joy of knowing that we defended His Word and lived His Word for His glory and the sake of those He has chosen.

---

8. *Luther's Works.* Weimar Edition. Briefwechsel [Correspondence], vol. 3, p 81f., as translated by Dr. Werner Gitt from the German.

Appendix 1 — The Survey

Aggregate Answers

(Note: This is a sampling of the questions and answers from the study. It is not comprehensive because of space limitations, and is taken from an 18-page summary compiled at the conclusion of the study. For clarity, the definition of these numerical columns and the methodology of their calculation is given below.)

Frequency is the actual number of people who gave a specific response to the question. Cumulative Frequency (CF) is equal to the total number of people who gave that response plus all prior responses to the question which adds up to the total number of interviews conducted. Percent represents the percentage of people who gave that specific response to a question. Cumulative Percent (CP) is equal to the total percentage of people who gave that response plus all prior responses to the question which adds up to 100 percent.

Age?	FREQUENCY	CF	PERCENT	CP
25–29	528	528	52.8	52.8
20–24	472	1000	47.2	100

Regularly attend church when growing up — but never/seldom go today?	FREQUENCY	CF	PERCENT	CP
Yes	1000	1000	100	100

IF REGULARLY ATTENDED — Which church denomination did you attend?	FREQUENCY	CF	PERCENT	CP
Baptist Church	260	260	26	26
Lutheran	136	396	13.6	39.6
Church of God	84	480	8.4	48
Christian Church	72	552	7.2	55.2
Pentecostal	69	621	6.9	62.1
Church of Christ	69	690	6.9	69
Assembly of God	66	756	6.6	75.6
Non-denominational	61	817	6.1	81.7
Presbyterian	44	861	4.4	86.1
Community Church	38	899	3.8	89.9
Calvary Chapel	32	931	3.2	93.1
Bible Church	29	960	2.9	96
Christian and Missionary Alliance	17	977	1.7	97.7
Evangelical Free Church	15	992	1.5	99.2
Brethren	8	1000	0.8	100

Did you attend church regularly during elementary/middle school years?

	FREQUENCY	CF	PERCENT	CP
Yes	946	946	94.6	94.6
No	54	1000	5.4	100

Did you attend church regularly during high school?

	FREQUENCY	CF	PERCENT	CP
Yes	561	561	56.1	56.1
No	439	1000	43.9	100

Did you attend church regularly throughout your college days?

	FREQUENCY	CF	PERCENT	CP
No	530	530	53	53
Did not attend college	356	886	35.6	88.6
Yes	114	1000	11.4	100

Why have you stopped attending church?	FREQUENCY	CF	PERCENT	CP
Boring service	119	119	11.9	11.9
Legalism	117	236	11.7	23.6
Hypocrisy — leaders	111	347	11.1	34.7
Too political	98	445	9.8	44.5
Self-righteous people	92	537	9.2	53.7
Distance from home	75	612	7.5	61.2
Not relevant personally	63	675	6.3	67.5
God would not condemn to hell	57	732	5.7	73.2
Bible not relevant	50	782	5	78.2
Not find preferred denomination in area	50	832	5	83.2
Not feel worthy	42	874	4.2	87.4
No time	29	903	2.9	90.3
Don't know	24	927	2.4	92.7
Hypocrisy — parents	20	947	2	94.7
Bible not true	16	963	1.6	96.3
Unfriendly people	11	974	1.1	97.4
Music is poor	10	984	1	98.4
Misc	6	990	0.6	99
Unsure my belief	5	995	0.5	99.5
Just quit going	3	998	0.3	99.8
Always ask for money	2	1000	0.2	100

Did you often attend Sunday school?	FREQUENCY	CF	PERCENT	CP
Yes	606	606	60.6	60.6
No	394	1000	39.4	100

IF OFTEN ATTENDED SUNDAY SCHOOL — Feel

Sunday school lessons were helpful?	FREQUENCY	CF	PERCENT	CP
Yes	436	436	71.95	71.95
No answer	394	436	0	71.95
No	114	550	18.81	90.76
Don't know	56	606	9.24	100

IF OFTEN ATTENDED SUNDAY SCHOOL — Did

you attend to see friends?	FREQUENCY	CF	PERCENT	CP
No answer	394	0	0	0
No	336	336	55.45	55.45
Yes	261	597	43.07	98.51
Don't know	9	606	1.49	100

IF OFTEN ATTENDED SUNDAY SCHOOL — Feel

lessons close to/different from school?	FREQUENCY	CF	PERCENT	CP
Very different	430	430	70.96	70.96
No answer	394	430	0	70.96
Close to what taught	176	606	29.04	100

IF OFTEN ATTENDED SUNDAY SCHOOL — Did

classes teach that Bible was true?	FREQUENCY	CF	PERCENT	CP
Yes	569	569	93.89	93.89
No answer	394	569	0	93.89
Don't know	32	601	5.28	99.17
No	5	606	0.83	100

IF OFTEN ATTENDED SUNDAY SCHOOL — Did

classes teach Bible could be defended?	FREQUENCY	CF	PERCENT	CP
No answer	394	0	0	0
Yes	344	344	56.77	56.77
No	167	511	27.56	84.32
Don't know	95	606	15.68	100

In high school, attend public/Christian/charter/home/Catholic?

	FREQUENCY	CF	PERCENT	CP
Public school	859	859	85.9	85.9
Christian school	69	928	6.9	92.8
Home school	34	962	3.4	96.2
Charter school	32	994	3.2	99.4
Catholic school	6	1000	0.6	100

Have instructors who taught that earth was millions of years old?

	FREQUENCY	CF	PERCENT	CP
Yes	785	785	78.5	78.5
No	192	977	19.2	97.7
Don't know	23	1000	2.3	100

Have instructors who taught that life evolved from lower forms?

	FREQUENCY	CF	PERCENT	CP
Yes	591	591	59.1	59.1
No	335	926	33.5	92.6
Don't know	74	1000	7.4	100

Because of school experience, leave high school believing Bible less true?

	FREQUENCY	CF	PERCENT	CP
No	670	670	67	67
Yes	278	948	27.8	94.8
Don't know	52	1000	5.2	100

Does the Bible contain errors?	FREQUENCY	CF	PERCENT	CP
Yes	397	397	39.7	39.7
Don't know	304	701	30.4	70.1
No	299	1000	29.9	100

IF CONTAINS ERRORS — Can you identify one of those errors for me?

	FREQUENCY	CF	PERCENT	CP
No answer	603	0	0	0
Alleged contradictions	88	88	22.17	22.17
Writers made mistake	73	161	18.39	40.55
Unsaved go to hell	64	225	16.12	56.68
No	51	276	12.85	69.52
Wrong about earth's age	40	316	10.08	79.6
Too much suffering and death	23	339	5.79	85.39

Genesis disproved by science	21	360	5.29	90.68
Miracles do not occur	10	370	2.52	93.2
Never was a global flood	8	378	2.02	95.21
Christ not really God	7	385	1.76	96.98
Trinity does not make sense	6	391	1.51	98.49
There is a hell	5	396	1.26	99.75
Misc	1	397	0.25	100

Do your parents still attend church regularly?	FREQUENCY	CF	PERCENT	CP
Yes	717	717	71.7	71.7
No	273	990	27.3	99
Don't know	10	1000	1	100

When you were younger, did your parents force you to go to church?	FREQUENCY	CF	PERCENT	CP
Yes	610	610	61	61
No	385	995	38.5	99.5
Don't know	5	1000	0.5	100

Do your closest friends attend church regularly right now?	FREQUENCY	CF	PERCENT	CP
No	649	649	64.9	64.9
Yes	337	986	33.7	98.6
Don't know	14	1000	1.4	100

Have any of your friends invited you to go back to church w/them?	FREQUENCY	CF	PERCENT	CP
No	505	505	50.5	50.5
Yes	479	984	47.9	98.4
Don't know	16	1000	1.6	100

Do you feel good people don't need to go to church?	FREQUENCY	CF	PERCENT	CP
No	562	562	56.2	56.2
Yes	352	914	35.2	91.4
Don't know	86	1000	8.6	100

Do you feel people w/college education less likely attend church?

	FREQUENCY	CF	PERCENT	CP
No	700	700	70	70
Yes	181	881	18.1	88.1
Don't know	119	1000	11.9	100

IF LESS LIKELY — Feel those w/college education influenced by professors?

	FREQUENCY	CF	PERCENT	CP
No answer	819	0	0	0
Yes	142	142	78.45	78.45
No	25	167	13.81	92.27
Don't know	14	181	7.73	100

Believe all the accounts/stories in the Bible are true/accurate?

	FREQUENCY	CF	PERCENT	CP
No	435	435	43.5	43.5
Yes	383	818	38.3	81.8
Don't know	182	1000	18.2	100

IF DON'T BELIEVE — What made you begin to doubt the Bible?

	FREQUENCY	CF	PERCENT	CP
No answer	565	0	0	0
Written by men	106	106	24.37	24.37
Not translated correctly	80	186	18.39	42.76
Contradicts itself	64	250	14.71	57.47
Science shows earth old	60	310	13.79	71.26
Bible has errors	48	358	11.03	82.3
Can't be a God with so much suffering	30	388	6.9	89.2
Christians don't live according to Bible	24	412	5.52	94.71
Evolution shows Bible cannot be trusted	19	431	4.37	99.08
Don't know	2	433	0.46	99.54
Misc	2	435	0.46	100

IF DON'T BELIEVE — When did you first have doubts?

	FREQUENCY	CF	PERCENT	CP
No answer	565	0	0	0
High school	190	190	43.68	43.68
Middle school	173	363	39.77	83.45
College	46	409	10.57	94.02
Elementary school	19	428	4.37	98.39
Don't know	7	435	1.61	100

Do you believe all the books of the Bible are inspired by God?

	FREQUENCY	CF	PERCENT	CP
Yes	617	617	61.7	61.7
No	211	828	21.1	82.8
Don't know	172	1000	17.2	100

Believe other holy books like the Koran are inspired by God?

	FREQUENCY	CF	PERCENT	CP
No	564	564	56.4	56.4
Don't know	291	855	29.1	85.5
Yes	145	1000	14.5	100

Believe in creation as stated in the Bible or in evolution?

	FREQUENCY	CF	PERCENT	CP
Biblical creation	718	718	71.8	71.8
Evolution	282	1000	28.2	100

Do you feel the Church is relevant to your needs today?

	FREQUENCY	CF	PERCENT	CP
Yes	469	469	46.9	46.9
No	437	906	43.7	90.6
Don't know	94	1000	9.4	100

IF NOT RELEVANT — In what way do you feel church is not fulfilling your needs?

	FREQUENCY	CF	PERCENT	CP
No answer	563	0	0	0
Not feeling closer to God there	143	143	32.72	32.72
Not practical	102	245	23.34	56.06
Not meeting emotional needs	95	340	21.74	77.8
Don't learn about more God	55	395	12.59	90.39
Not establishing friendships at church	18	413	4.12	94.51
Bible not true	10	423	2.29	96.8
Don't know	6	429	1.37	98.17
Misc	6	435	1.37	99.54
Not telling truth there	2	437	0.46	100

Do you believe in the creation of Adam & Eve and Garden of Eden?

	FREQUENCY	CF	PERCENT	CP
Yes	749	749	74.9	74.9
No	186	935	18.6	93.5
Don't know	65	1000	6.5	100

Believe Adam & Eve sinned and were expelled from the Garden?	FREQUENCY	CF	PERCENT	CP
YES	748	748	74.8	74.8
No	165	913	16.5	91.3
Don't know	87	1000	8.7	100

Believe in story of Sodom & Gomorrah — Lot's wife turned to salt?	FREQUENCY	CF	PERCENT	CP
Yes	618	618	61.8	61.8
No	256	874	25.6	87.4
Don't know	126	1000	12.6	100

Do you believe in Noah's ark and the global Flood?	FREQUENCY	CF	PERCENT	CP
Yes	773	773	77.3	77.3
No	153	926	15.3	92.6
Don't know	74	1000	7.4	100

Do you believe there was a Tower of Babel as recorded in Genesis?	FREQUENCY	CF	PERCENT	CP
Yes	631	631	63.1	63.1
No	196	827	19.6	82.7
Don't know	173	1000	17.3	100

Do you believe the earth is less than 10,000 years old?	FREQUENCY	CF	PERCENT	CP
No	571	571	57.1	57.1
Don't know	224	795	22.4	79.5
Yes	205	1000	20.5	100

Has secular science dating the earth 6 billion years caused you to doubt Bible?	FREQUENCY	CF	PERCENT	CP
Yes	464	464	46.4	46.4
No	424	888	42.4	88.8
Don't know	112	1000	11.2	100

Believe that God used evolution to change one kind of animal to another?	FREQUENCY	CF	PERCENT	CP
No	562	562	56.2	56.2
Yes	239	801	23.9	80.1
Don't know	199	1000	19.9	100

Do you believe that humans evolved from an ape-like ancestor?

	FREQUENCY	CF	PERCENT	CP
No	543	543	54.3	54.3
Yes	301	844	30.1	84.4
Don't know	156	1000	15.6	100

Do you believe God used evolution to create human beings?

	FREQUENCY	CF	PERCENT	CP
No	608	608	60.8	60.8
Yes	222	830	22.2	83
Don't know	170	1000	17	100

Did pastor/Sunday school teacher teach Christians could believe Darwin?

	FREQUENCY	CF	PERCENT	CP
No	789	789	78.9	78.9
Don't know	116	905	11.6	90.5
Yes	95	1000	9.5	100

Ever teach that Christians could believe earth millions/billions years old?

	FREQUENCY	CF	PERCENT	CP
No	592	592	59.2	59.2
Yes	266	858	26.6	85.8
Don't know	142	1000	14.2	100

Ever teach that God created earth in six days, each 24 hours long?

	FREQUENCY	CF	PERCENT	CP
Yes	826	826	82.6	82.6
No	110	936	11	93.6
Don't know	64	1000	6.4	100

Ever teach that the Book of Genesis was a myth or legend?

	FREQUENCY	CF	PERCENT	CP
No	857	857	85.7	85.7
Don't know	76	933	7.6	93.3
Yes	67	1000	6.7	100

Believe Joseph was sold into slavery & became Pharaoh's closest advisor?

	FREQUENCY	CF	PERCENT	CP
Yes	534	534	53.4	53.4
Don't know	264	798	26.4	79.8
No	202	1000	20.2	100

Is there one idea you question more than the rest?

	FREQUENCY	CF	PERCENT	CP
No	415	415	41.5	41.5
Earth is young not old	298	713	29.8	71.3
Days of creation were 24-hour days	134	847	13.4	84.7
Really was Adam/Eve	116	963	11.6	96.3
Really was Noah's Flood	37	1000	3.7	100

Would you say questioning was beginning of your doubt in the Bible?

	FREQUENCY	CF	PERCENT	CP
No answer	412	0	0	0
Yes	327	327	55.61	55.61
No	183	510	31.12	86.73
Don't know	78	588	13.27	100

At what age did you begin to really question contents in Bible?

	FREQUENCY	CF	PERCENT	CP
High school years	457	457	45.7	45.7
Grades 7–9	293	750	29.3	75
Grades 4–6	128	878	12.8	87.8
Early college	112	990	11.2	99
Grades K–3	10	1000	1	100

Anything a teacher did/said that caused you to doubt the Bible?

	FREQUENCY	CF	PERCENT	CP
No	728	728	72.8	72.8
Evolution was true	119	847	11.9	84.7
Bible was attacked	60	907	6	90.7
Christians are hypocrites	38	945	3.8	94.5
Don't know	31	976	3.1	97.6
Atheism was true	9	985	0.9	98.5
Christians want to take over society	8	993	0.8	99.3
God described as unloving	7	1000	0.7	100

Did your parents' behavior influence you not to attend church?

	FREQUENCY	CF	PERCENT	CP
No	774	774	77.4	77.4
Yes	201	975	20.1	97.5
Don't know	25	1000	2.5	100

Do you expect to attend church regularly after you have children?

	FREQUENCY	CF	PERCENT	CP
Yes	381	381	38.1	38.1
No	322	703	32.2	70.3
Don't know	297	1000	29.7	100

IF ANY DENOMINATION — Why do you expect to attend this denomination?

	FREQUENCY	CF	PERCENT	CP
No answer	627	0	0	0
One I grew up with	170	170	45.58	45.58
Closest to my beliefs	116	286	31.1	76.68
Heard good things	30	316	8.04	84.72
Large denomination in area	29	345	7.77	92.49
Friend/relative is part of denomination	28	373	7.51	100

Do you attend any church services at Easter or Christmas?

	FREQUENCY	CF	PERCENT	CP
No	492	492	49.2	49.2
Both	235	727	23.5	72.7
Easter	163	890	16.3	89
Christmas	110	1000	11	100

IF DO NOT ATTEND — In what way do you view church today?

	FREQUENCY	CF	PERCENT	CP
No answer	508	0	0	0
Don't think of it at all	182	182	36.99	36.99
Hypocritical	89	271	18.09	55.08
Too political	69	340	14.02	69.11
Irrelevant	52	392	10.57	79.67
Boring	40	432	8.13	87.8
Caring	28	460	5.69	93.5
Social club	16	476	3.25	96.75
Loving environment	15	491	3.05	99.8
Misc	1	492	0.2	100

Is there any part of the church service that you miss today?

	FREQUENCY	CF	PERCENT	CP
Yes	500	500	50	50
No	454	954	45.4	95.4
Don't know	46	1000	4.6	100

IF MISS ANY PART - Which part do you still miss?	FREQUENCY	CF	PERCENT	CP
No answer	500	0	0	0
Worshiping God	103	103	20.6	20.6
Special events	96	199	19.2	39.8
Pastor's teaching	93	292	18.6	58.4
Outreach to community	77	369	15.4	73.8
Friends	68	437	13.6	87.4
Music	35	472	7	94.4
Sunday school class	27	499	5.4	99.8
Misc	1	500	0.2	100

Do you believe you are saved and will go to heaven upon death?	FREQUENCY	CF	PERCENT	CP
Yes	656	656	65.6	65.6
Don't know	208	864	20.8	86.4
No	136	1000	13.6	100

Do you believe you have become anti-church through the years?	FREQUENCY	CF	PERCENT	CP
No	608	608	60.8	60.8
Yes	343	951	34.3	95.1
Don't know	49	1000	4.9	100

Which of these make you question the Bible most?	FREQUENCY	CF	PERCENT	CP
None	326	326	32.6	32.6
Earth not less than10,000 years old	250	576	25	57.6
Too many rules	128	704	12.8	70.4
Creation account	121	825	12.1	82.5
Bible does not make sense of suffering/death	111	936	11.1	93.6
Miracles not true	29	965	2.9	96.5
Flood of Noah	24	989	2.4	98.9
Christ's divinity	11	1000	1.1	100

Is gay marriage morally acceptable?	FREQUENCY	CF	PERCENT	CP
No	741	741	74.1	74.1
Yes	164	905	16.4	90.5
Don't know	95	1000	9.5	100

Should abortion continue to be legal in most instances?

	FREQUENCY	CF	PERCENT	CP
No	488	488	48.8	48.8
Yes	380	868	38	86.8
Don't know	132	1000	13.2	100

Should science instructors be allowed to teach problems w/evolution?

	FREQUENCY	CF	PERCENT	CP
Yes	517	517	51.7	51.7
No	312	829	31.2	82.9
Don't know	171	1000	17.1	100

Should prayer be allowed in public schools?	FREQUENCY	CF	PERCENT	CP
Yes	718	718	71.8	71.8
No	178	896	17.8	89.6
Don't know	104	1000	10.4	100

Is premarital sex okay?	FREQUENCY	CF	PERCENT	CP
Yes	517	517	51.7	51.7
No	435	952	43.5	95.2
Don't know	48	1000	4.8	100

What is your family status?	FREQUENCY	CF	PERCENT	CP
Married/children	387	387	38.7	38.7
Single	296	683	29.6	68.3
Married	262	945	26.2	94.5
Single/children	55	1000	5.5	100

IF MARRIED — Were you married in a church?	FREQUENCY	CF	PERCENT	CP
Yes	454	454	69.95	69.95
No Answer	351	454	0	69.95
No	195	649	30.05	100

What is the last grade of school you have completed?

	FREQUENCY	CF	PERCENT	CP
HS graduate	362	362	36.2	36.2
College graduate	328	690	32.8	69
Some college	256	946	25.6	94.6
Graduate school	44	990	4.4	99
Less than HS	10	1000	1	100

Combined income?

	FREQUENCY	CF	PERCENT	CP
$50,000–$74,999	303	303	30.3	30.3
$36,000–$49,999	267	570	26.7	57
$24,000–$35,999	265	835	26.5	83.5
$15,000–$23,999	119	954	11.9	95.4
$75,000 and up	28	982	2.8	98.2
$6,000–$14,999	13	995	1.3	99.5
Under $6,000	5	1000	0.5	100

What is the occupation of the head of the household?

	FREQUENCY	CF	PERCENT	CP
Blue collar	454	454	45.4	45.4
White collar	442	896	44.2	89.6
Government/military	52	948	5.2	94.8
Self-employed	41	989	4.1	98.9
Student/homemaker	9	998	0.9	99.8
Unemployed	2	1000	0.2	100

Location?	FREQUENCY	CF	PERCENT	CP
South Atlantic	180	180	18	18
E. North Central	170	350	17	35
Pacific	160	510	16	51
Middle	150	660	15	66
W. South Central	100	760	10	76
W. North Central	70	830	7	83
E. South Central	60	890	6	89
Mountain	60	950	6	95
New England	50	1000	5	100

Appendix 2 — The 15 Questions of Life

Can your child, your student or your church family answer the following questions?

In 1 Peter 3:15, God reveals the importance of being able to defend our belief in Christ, and as believers we do not need to fear engaging the culture of disbelief with the truth of God's purpose and vision for our lives.

Discover vital answers and starting points for these issues at:
www.answersingenesis.org/go/questionsoflife

1. Why am I here?
2. Who is God?
3. Who is Jesus and why is He the only path to salvation?
4. Why the Bible and not other holy books?
5. Why should the Bible be the authority in my life when making decisions and moral choices?
6. Why set boundaries on sexuality and marriage?
7. If we are descendents of one man and one woman where did all the different races come from?
8. How does one determine the value of a human life?
9. Dinosaurs and the Bible – how does that work?
10. What is wrong with the world (suffering and death) when God supposedly made everything perfect?
11. How can "what is wrong with the world" be made right?
12. Does "science" disprove or confirm history in the Bible?
13. Why does the age of the earth really matter to me and my life today?
14. Why is it important that I believe in a literal 6-day, 24-hour creation?
15. Did we evolve from apes-like creatures?

Appendix 3 — Resources for Upholding the Word

Books

- *More Than a Carpenter*, by Josh McDowell (Wheaton, IL: Tyndale House Publishers, 1977)
- *Always Ready*, by Greg Bahnsen (Powder Springs, GA: American Vision, 1996)
- *The Ultimate Proof of Creation*, by Jason Lisle (Green Forest, AR: Master Books, 2009)
- *The New Answers Book*, Vol. 1 and 2, Ken Ham, general editor (Green Forest, AR: Master Books, 2007 & 2008)
- *Ask Them Why*, by Jay Lucas (Schaumburg, IL: Regular Baptist Press, 2007)
- *Nothing but the Truth*, by Brian Edwards (Darlington, England: Evangelical Press, 2006)
- *The Young Earth*, by John Morris (Green Forest, AR: Master Books, 2007)
- *How Could a Loving God . . . ?* by Ken Ham (Green Forest, AR: Master Books, 2007)
- *The Answers Book for Kids*, Vols. 1, 2, 3, and 4, Ken Ham, editor (Green Forest, AR: Master Books, 2008)
- *The Long War Against God*, by Henry M. Morris (Green Forest, AR: Master Books, 2000)

Online Education

- Answers Education Online through Answers in Genesis website: answersingenesis.org/cec/courses/

Websites

- Answersingenesis.org
- ICR.org
- Creationresearch.org
- Christiananswers.net
- Masterbooks.net

DVDs

- Creation mini-series, Ken Ham (Answers in Genesis)
- How Do We Know the Bible Is True? Brian Edwards
- Creation: Science Confirms the Bible Is True, Jason Lisle (Answers in Genesis)
- God of Suffering, Tommy Mitchell (Answers in Genesis)
- Noah's Flood: Washing Away Millions of Years, Terry Mortenson (Answers in Genesis)
- Demolishing Strongholds DVD Curriculum (Answers in Genesis)

Appendix 4 — Resources for Parents

- *Raising Godly Children*, Ken Ham (Green Forest, AR: Master Books, 2008)
- *History Revealed Curriculum*, Diana Waring (Answers in Genesis)
- *Answers* Magazine: answersingenesis.org/articles/am
- God's Design Science Curriculum Set (Answers in Genesis)
- Bring your family to the Creation Museum.
- Answers in Genesis website: answersingenesis.org
- Genesis: Key to Reclaiming the Culture DVD, Ken Ham
- *The New Answers Book*, Vol. 1 and 2, Ken Ham, general editor (Green Forest, AR: Master Books)
- *The Lie: Evolution,* Ken Ham (Green Forest, AR: Master Books, 1987)
- Master Books website: masterbooks.net

Appendix 5 — Resources for Christian Educators

- Genesis: Key to Reclaiming the Culture DVD, Ken Ham (Answers in Genesis)
- History Revealed Curriculum (Answers in Genesis)
- *Noah's Ark, Thinking Outside the Box,* Tim Lovett (Green Forest, AR: Master Books, 2008)
- *Taking Back Astronomy,* Jason Lisle (Green Forest, AR: Master Books, 2006)
- *Answers* Magazine: answersingenesis.org/articles/am
- God's Design Science Curriculum Set (Answers in Genesis)
- Answers in Genesis website: answersingenesis.org (For the technical minded, see the Answers In-Depth section, Answers Research Journal at answersingenesis.org/arj, and the many technical books available through the website.)
- Demolishing Strongholds Curriculum Set (Answers in Genesis)
- *New Answers Book,* Vol. 1 and 2, Ken Ham, general editor (Green Forest, AR: Master Books, 2007 & 2008)
- *Adam's Wall Chart of World History* (Green Forest, AR: Master Books, 2007)
- *Annals of the World,* James Ussher (Green Forest, AR: Master Books, 2003)
- *Chronology of the Old Testament,* Floyd Jones (Green Forest, AR: Master Books, 2005)
- *Evolution Exposed,* Vol. 1 and 2 (essential for high school students and extremely helpful for educators), Roger Patterson (Answers in Genesis, 2007)
- *Old Earth Creationism on Trial,* Jason Lisle and Tim Chaffey (Green Forest, AR: Master Books, 2008)
- Master Books website: masterbooks.net

Appendix 6 — Resources for Youth Pastors

- *The Long War Against God*, by Henry M. Morris (Green Forest, AR: Master Books, 2000)
- Demolishing Strongholds DVD Curriculum (Answers in Genesis)
- *The Great Dinosaur Mystery Solved*, Ken Ham (Green Forest, AR: Master Books, 1998)
- The Bible Explains Dinosaurs DVD, Ken Ham (Answers in Genesis)
- Best Evidence DVD (Answers in Genesis)
- Bring youth groups to the Creation Museum.
- God of Suffering DVD, Tommy Mitchell (Answers in Genesis)
- Only One Race DVD, Ken Ham (Answers in Genesis)
- *Answers Books for Kids* series (for younger kids) (Green Forest, AR: Master Books, 2008)
- It All Begins with Genesis Curriculum (Jr high and up) (Answers in Genesis)
- Answers for Kids website: answersingenesis.org/kids
- Genesis: Key to Reclaiming the Culture DVD, Ken Ham (Answers in Genesis)
- *New Answers Book*, Vol. 1 and 2, Ken Ham, general editor (great for teens and up)(Green Forest, AR: Master Books, 2007 & 2008)
- *Adam's Wall Chart of World History* (Green Forest, AR: Master Books, 2007)
- *Creation: Facts of Life*, Gary Parker (great for teens and up) (Green Forest, AR: Master Books, 1980)
- *Evolution Exposed, Vol. 1 and 2* (essential for high school students) (Answers in Genesis)
- Created Cosmos DVD (Junior level and up) (Answers in Genesis)

Appendix 7 — Resources for Pastors

- *New Answers Book* Vol. 1 and 2, Ken Ham, general editor (Green Forest, AR: Master Books)

- *Coming to Grips with Genesis*, Terry Mortenson, Ph.D., Thane H. Ury, Ph.D, editors (Green Forest, AR: Master Books, 2008)

- *The Genesis Record*, Dr. Henry Morris (commentary on Genesis) (Grand Rapids, MI: Baker Book House, 1976)

- *Creation and Change*, Doug Kelly (Scotland, UK: Christian Focus Publications, 2003)

- *Old Earth Creationism on Trial*, Jason Lisle and Tim Chaffey (Green Forest, AR: Master Books, 2008)

- *Why Won't They Listen?* Ken Ham (Green Forest, AR: Master Books, 2002)

- Genesis: Key to Reclaiming the Culture DVD, Ken Ham

- Why Won't They Listen? DVD, Ken Ham (Answers in Genesis)

- Creation Mini-series, Ken Ham (DVD set includes Why Won't They Listen? and Genesis: Key to Reclaiming the Culture) (Answers in Genesis)

- *The Annals of the World,* James Ussher — for reference (Green Forest, AR: Master Books, 2003)

- *The Complete Works of Flavius Josephus* — for reference (Green Forest, AR: Master Books, 2008)

- *The Ultimate Proof of Creation* Jason Lisle (Green Forest, AR: Master Books, 2009)

- Organize a church trip to the Creation Museum.

- Answers Vacation Bible School sets (available on the Answers in Genesis website)

- Answers in Genesis website: answersingenesis.org

Ken Ham

The president/CEO and founder of Answers in Genesis-U.S. and the highly acclaimed Creation Museum, Ken Ham is one of the most in-demand Christian speakers in North America. Ham, a native Australian now residing near Cincinnati, Ohio, is the author of numerous books on the Book of Genesis, the accuracy and authority of the Bible, dinosaurs, and the destructive fruits of evolutionary thinking (including his co-authored book on the "races" and racism, *Darwin's Plantation*, and the bestseller, *The Lie: Evolution*). He appears frequently on American TV (in one year alone: Fox's The O'Reilly Factor and Fox and Friends in the Morning, CNN's The Situation Room with Wolf Blitzer, ABC's Good Morning America, the BBC radio/TV, and others).

Ken hosts the daily radio program "Answers . . . with Ken Ham," heard on more than 800 stations in America (and dozens more overseas) and is one of the editors and contributing authors for AIG's *Answers* magazine (a biblical worldview publication with over 70,000 worldwide subscribers). The new high-tech Creation Museum near the Cincinnati Airport — which attracted over 700,000 visitors (and several of the world's major media) in its first two and a half years of operation — was Ken's brainchild.

C. Britt Beemer

Britt Beemer holds a BA from Northwest Missouri State University and has an MA from Indiana State University. He worked for Congressman Bill Scherle (R-IA) from 1966–1974. After his work with Congressman Scherle, he was a senior research analyst for the Heritage Foundation. He then began to manage and conduct 14 senatorial campaigns, which included exacting research and demanding strategic planning.

In 1979, Beemer founded America's Research Group, a full-service consumer behavior research and strategic marketing firm. Recognized nationally as a premier marketing strategist, he has gained wide acclaim for his work on how, when, and why consumers select their products and services. His client list represents America's top retailers, leading brands, and smaller entrepreneurial companies. His knowledge of consumer preferences increases monthly as ARG conducts thousands of new interviews.

His work has been cited in the media, including the *Wall Street Journal*, the *New York Times, Investor's Business Daily, CNN, Fox News, Fox Business News*, and many others.

He is the author of *Predatory Marketing*, a book on strategic marketing. His second book, *It Takes a Prophet to Make a Profit*, is about emerging trends of the millennium. *The Customer Rules*, released in 2008, details how customer-focused businesses win.

Britt Beemer's expertise covers each phase of survey research, including questionnaire design, sample construction, and data analysis, but especially interpretation. He serves as the senior director of research at America's Research Group, where he personally reviews all research and prepares and presents each strategic marketing plan.

Todd Hillard

Todd Hillard is a freelance writer from San Antonio, Texas, where he lives with his wife and five kids. A former youth pastor and missionary, he is passionate about taking the dreams and stories of others and bringing them to life on the written page.

Todd was born and raised in the Black Hills of South Dakota. He received his BS in pre-med studies and psychology from the University of Utah and his MA in English from Arizona State University. He and his family lived in Turkey for two and a half years. He has 17 years of pastoral experience and has written more than 12 books.

Demolishing Strongholds
TEEN/ADULT STUDY KIT

Inspire your group to go to the next level in their Christian walk! Challenge them to live out their faith with this comprehensive 13-session DVD-based study. *Demolishing Strongholds* features Ken Ham and three other excellent speakers who address strategic topics, such as developing a biblical worldview, how to engage and reach friends for Christ, confidence-boosting ideas on how to confront our evolutionized culture, examples of "cultural brainwashing," and an inspiring challenge on how to be God's players in the game called life. *Includes: 13 DVDs, teacher/student study guides, and inductive Bible study kit. Audience: Adults & Teens*

www.DemolishingStrongholds.com

Raising Godly Children in an Ungodly World

Ken Ham and Steve Ham

Christian families are struggling in a culture hostile to Christian values, and increasingly find themselves searching for answers and strategies to be more effective. Parents also face a disturbing trend of young people leaving home and leaving the Church — and want to ensure their children have a strong foundation of biblical faith and understanding. Discover how to create an incredible faith legacy in your family! *Raising Godly Children in an Ungodly World* presents empowering insight for:

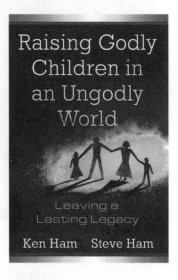

- Surviving the culture wars as a family
- Educating children — the Bible offers guidance
- Practical tips for raising spiritually healthy children
- Solutions to the root cause of dysfunctional families
- Discovering biblical authority as a parent
- Discipline — necessary and lovingly administered

Ken Ham is joined by his brother, Steve Ham, in presenting this powerful look at how the principles and truth of Genesis are vital to the strong and lasting foundation of a family. Sharing their own stories of growing up in a "Genesis" family and sharing this legacy within their own families, it is an intensely personal and practical guide for parents.

Master Books®
A Division of New Leaf Publishing Group
www.masterbooks.net

paperback • 240 pages • $12.99
ISBN-13: 978-0-89051-542-6
ISBN-10: 0-89051-542-5

Available at Christian bookstores nationwide or www.nlpg.com